Looking For Love

Looking For Love

A Life Transformed

**Maureen Sims
with
Jenny Roberts**

Marshall Pickering

Marshall Morgan and Scott,
Marshall Pickering
34–42 Cleveland Street, London, W1P 5FB, U.K.

First published in 1990 by Marshall Morgan and Scott
Publications Ltd
Part of the Marshall Pickering Holdings Group

British Library Cataloguing in Publication Data
Sims, Maureen
  Looking for love
  1. Christian life. Biographies
  I. Title
  248.4'092'4

ISBN 0-551-01967-0

Text set in Bembo by Selectmove Ltd, London
Printed in Great Britain by
Cox & Wyman Ltd, Reading, Berks.

Contents

Foreword
Preface 9
 1. The child 12
 2. The teenager 22
 3. The wife 33
 4. Ron 48
 5. On the site 54
 6. Anguished years 70
 7. Heartache 83
 8. A new creation 97
 9. Cancer 110
10. Stepping out in boldness 119
11. A woman of faith 131

Foreword

There are lots of Christian autobiographies about. So why another one? The short answer is because Maureen Sims's story adds a unique dimension to the annals of Christian testimony to the astonishing grace of God.

Raw but poignant, it graphically tells of the severe examination of human weakness and strength. This is a record of God-breathed triumph without a trace of triumphalism for truly, as Maureen's life today bears eloquent witness, God has faithfully 'restored the years' which the storming locusts have eaten'. We read of God's healing, recreating power. From the ashes of abject degradation and bitterness rises a gentle trophy of divine grace.

After reading this gripping story, you will rejoice with the new creation who now stands tall in the Jesus who has rescued her. With Maureen Sims you too will exclaim: 'Hallelujah, What a Saviour!'

Shirley Martin
Trevor and Shirley Martin
Ministries
Dorking
Surrey

Preface

My story is not an easy one to tell. There have been many periods of my life that I would rather forget, many episodes that are distressing for me to dwell on. So why am I telling my story here? Why delve back into memories that can only cause me pain?

First, I am telling my story because I believe that is what God would have me do. I believe that he wants to use my story to give hope to others. I know how much hurt and how much pain there is in the world today; how many people long for comfort and peace in their lives. I know how much evil there is in the world; how many people are trapped and desperately looking for a way out. I have been through the pain and the fear and the desperation and I have found a way out. I want people to know about the life I lived and the life I have now so that they can see that there can be new life for anyone, whatever their past has been.

Jesus Christ has made me a new creation. The Maureen Sims who is telling you this story is not the same Maureen Sims that existed before the Lord came into my life and changed it.

Before I became a Christian I would find it hard to talk even to one person. Just an ordinary conversation was agony for me. People might come to our house and spend a whole evening with us and the only words I would utter would be 'hello' and 'goodbye'. Now I can talk boldly and fearlessly to congregations of over a thousand people. It wasn't just that I was shy before – though I certainly was painfully shy. I couldn't talk to people because I had nothing to say to them. My head was empty.

I was a person with no views, no opinions, no mind of my own – just an emptiness to be filled with whatever the world fed me. Now Jesus has given me something to say and I long to tell as many people as possible what he has done for me and what he can do for them. Once my empty mind was a channel for evil; now I have become a channel for the power of God's Holy Spirit.

Before I became a Christian my marriage was in ruins. It had become a hell, a nightmare, where love had turned into hatred, and I could see no way out but suicide. Before my husband accepted Jesus he was violent, destructive, a man with no principles and no tenderness. Now the love of God shines through him. We have joy and love in our marriage and in our family. Christ had made us one.

Once I was friendless and alone. I was leading an evil life that brought me no happiness, but one that I was unable to abandon. I took refuge in drink, in drugs. I mixed with criminals and was driven to prostitution. Today I have a happy, peaceful life with many loving friends, but I still mix with criminals, alcoholics, drug addicts and prostitutes. These are people I can identify with because I have been there myself. I talk often to people in prison; I have addicts and prostitutes in my house, and I tell them about the love of Jesus, which can rescue them as it did me.

Jesus is real. I know that he is real because if he hadn't come into my life I would now be either dead or in a mental institution. Whoever changed me from the lifeless, hopeless zombie that I was then to the woman I am now just has to be real. So many people say 'How I wish I could have my life over again!' They can! Whatever their needs, whatever their pain, whatever mess they have made of their lives, people can start them all over again as new creations. But there is only one way out, only one way forward. Jesus is peace; Jesus is love; Jesus is comfort. Nobody can do without him.

I will never turn away from the love of God because I know that without it I am nothing. God has given me my loving husband, my secure family, my health, my life. So many people today are going through the sort of experiences that I once knew. If, by reading my story, just one such person might find the way out – the joy and blessings of new life in Jesus – then telling it will have been worthwhile.

1: The child

I was a war baby. My parents lived in Battersea but, in 1944, when my mother was expecting me, London was a dangerous place to be living. So my mother was evacuated to Woking, in Surrey, and that's where I was born.

I think of my childhood as a fairly normal and secure one. Certainly I cannot make the excuse that all the things I did wrong were due to an unhappy or deprived childhood. We were not rich, but we lived comfortably. I felt loved by my parents. And though I was an only child, my parents both came from large families so I had a whole army of cousins.

When I was born my father was in the air force. But when the war ended he returned to his pre-war occupation of chef. He was head chef at the Cumberland, a big hotel in the West End of London. I was proud to have a father with such an important job, and I used to love hearing his stories about the grand occasions he catered for and the famous people who came into the hotel. The catering for Ascot was done at the hotel, and my father would describe the rich racegoers in their smart clothes and fancy hats – it all seemed like another world to me. What I didn't realise was that the glamour and luxury of a top hotel doesn't extend beyond the kitchen door. My father worked very long hours and the work was exhausting. His health began to suffer. He became very run down, was always tired, and suffered constantly from boils. Eventually he had to give up the job and took on a new one as a driver for a laundry. His round included deliveries to hotels and to big private houses, so he had not moved entirely away from the world of the rich.

My father was a quiet man, gentle and thoughtful. He loved his garden, and most of his leisure time was taken up with working in it. He wasn't mean but he was careful with his money. Every Friday night he would sit down and work out his accounts of everything he'd earned and spent that week, down to the last penny. He was a kind, considerate husband, always willing to help with cleaning the house, and cooking the dinner on his day off.

My mother stayed at home to look after me until I went to school. Then she took a job at an open-air school on Clapham Common. It was a school for children who had learning difficulties and deprived backgrounds. They had all their meals in the school, and my mother worked in the kitchen there. She was a sociable, outgoing person, who liked to go out and have a good time. She was always the life and soul of every party, singing, dancing, and playing the piano. I remember my parents going out a lot, dancing or drinking, and looking back I believe this must have been what my mother wanted, rather than my father. I think he would probably have been happy to stay in quietly every evening.

I suppose I sometimes resented my parents going out, and would have liked them always to stay at home with me. There are two occasions that have stayed in my memory when I really did feel neglected. Once, when I was just a toddler of two or three my parents went out for a drink. I woke up in my cot and called out but nobody came. I got up and wandered tearfully around the house looking for my parents but the house was empty. Then I must have made my way to the front door and opened it. Perhaps I thought of going to look for my parents, but was frightened to go out into the dark night. Then a man passed by and saw me.

'What's the matter, love?' he asked.

'I want my Mum and Dad.'

'Where are they, then?'

'There're down the pub,' I howled. This stranger took pity on me and went straight down to the pub to fetch my parents, and I was soon comforted.

The other incident was when my parents went out, leaving me with a young cousin, although I had been complaining of pains in my stomach. The pains turned out to be appendicitis and because of the delay in getting me to hospital I developed peritonitis and very nearly died.

These are isolated incidents, though, and I did not think of myself as a neglected child. We were a close family and always did things together, going out for walks or visiting relatives. My parents were very fond of each other and neither of them ever did anything without the other. Perhaps they were so wrapped up in each other that they did not have quite enough love and time left for me. That's how it looks to me now, but I didn't think like that at the time. I felt secure in the love of my parents, particularly my father, who was an affectionate man. But we weren't a family who were physically demonstrative. Although my parents loved each other I never saw them kiss or cuddle. My mother sometimes said, 'I wish Jim would just hold my hand or take my arm when we're out together.' I, too, would have welcomed more cuddling.

My childhood memories are bound up with the houses in which we lived. My mother returned to Battersea shortly after I was born. We lived in two rooms in a big old-fashioned house with high ceilings and large windows. The rooms were drab, damp and cold, and we didn't have a great deal of furniture. But it was clean. It must have been miserable for my mother in those last months of the war, sitting alone in those bleak rooms, with blackout curtains drawn, listening to the air-raid sirens and to the wails of her baby. For I was a baby who cried day and night.

When my father returned from the air force it became impossibly crowded in two rooms and eventually we moved to a larger house, just on the edge of Clapham Common. This was a terraced house with five bedrooms and quite a large garden. As I remember the house, childhood memories come flooding back.

I remember the living room where we used to sit in the evenings listening to the radio: 'Journey into Space' or 'The Archers'. My mother would often be knitting. This was one of her hobbies, and I always had hand-knitted jumpers and cardigans. We only used the room we called 'the best room' on Sundays and special occasions. On Sundays we nearly always went out for a walk, and then came a lazy afternoon in front of the fire in the best room. I remember sitting and picking at the bone from Sunday lunch while Mum toasted crumpets by the fire.

The scullery was where all the washing was done. There was a big stone boiler, and once a week my mother would spend most of the day there, scrubbing away at her washboard. We didn't have a bathroom, so this was where our bathing took place too, every Friday night. We had something called a 'bungalow bath' which had to be pushed out into the garden to be emptied.

My bedroom was a small room and I sometimes slept in the living room. But wherever I slept I was never free from night terrors. I was almost literally frightened of my own shadow. There was a tree outside the house, and a street lamp, and between them they cast shadows on the wall that became the stuff of nightmares to me. My cousin Carol used to stay with us often and it was her delight to tease me. Knowing how nervous I was, she would pretend to see all kinds of horrors and apparitions, and I was all too ready to believe her.

My aunt had a flat at the top of the house. Besides my Mum and Dad she was the person I loved best in the world. I felt sorry for her because she seemed so lonely. She worked during the day, but she spent her evenings and weekends alone. I spent a lot of time up in her flat and always stayed with her when my parents went out on a Saturday night. I was never a child who found conversation easy, but I could talk to my aunt. I think I talked to her more than I did to my parents, and in many ways I was like a daughter to her.

Our garden, lovingly tended by my father, was quite large, though it was overlooked by neighbouring gardens. I remember looking over the wall into another garden where a little boy about my age lived. He often had friends in and then I would just stand and watch them playing. They never invited me to join them and if they had I would have been too shy to do so. But I envied this boy who had so many friends and so many toys. When he was alone I had the courage to talk to him and I'm afraid most of my conversation was lies.

'I'm going to the circus next week,' I might say. 'And last week my auntie took me out to this big hotel and we had strawberries and cream from gold dishes.'

'Look at my new Meccano set,' he would say.

'That's nothing,' I'd reply. 'I've got a bigger Meccano set than that. And I've got a doll who can walk and talk and she's got a dress made out of silk, and a velvet cloak.'

I don't know why I had to invent all these things. It wasn't as though I was actually short of real outings and toys, even if they might not have been as grand as those of my fantasies. Our extended family was so large that there were always relatives to invite or to visit. Every other Sunday we went for lunch and tea to my aunt and uncle's house; they were the parents of my cousin Carol. This was a different cousin called Carol, not the one who liked to frighten me. I remember going there after my aunt had had her second child. I couldn't bear to hear the baby cry. It would make me cry too, so my aunt would be forced to pick her up.

Christmas was always a happy time, when the house was full of our relatives. Some of my cousins always stayed overnight and we would put out pillow cases on Christmas Eve for Father Christmas to fill. The aunts and uncles all brought presents and there would be a party where my uncle would dress as Father Christmas and give all the children presents from the tree.

Another treat was meeting my father from work on a Sunday. Some Sunday mornings Mum would say, 'Go and put your best clothes on, we're going on the bus to meet your Dad.' She never needed to ask me twice. I loved the bus journey to the West End, and it was exciting to meet my father at that huge hotel and to know that he belonged to such a grand and impressive place. We used to walk around Hyde Park together, then drive home. Later in the day we would sometimes go to Clapham Common where a band played.

There were happy times but I cannot really say I was a happy child. I was always so quiet and nervous, and never found it easy to make friends. I was so shy when I was very young that if anyone came to our house I used to hide under the table. I loved my parents but there were tensions between us. My mother always seemed to be on at me about one thing or another. When we were alone together I was not much company for her. I never had much conversation. I think I must have got on her nerves. I remember her often saying, 'For goodness sake, Maureen, can't you find yourself something to do? Why can't you go out? I'm tired of having you always under my feet.' But I was afraid to go out. I used to stand at the window and watch other children playing but I would not go out to join them. I was afraid they would hit me or laugh at me or abuse me.

My mother was always scolding me for being lazy and not helping her, and not tidying my bedroom. When I became a mother myself I understood how she felt. But at the time I was upset and hated it when she shouted at me. My father always used to take my part. My mother has told me since that the only arguments they ever had were over me, and it was always my father who was the soft one. I suppose I was a real 'Daddy's girl'.

Even with my father, though we had a loving relationship, I was unable to talk. I never told either of my parents about my night fears or about Carol's teasing. The few times I actually called to my mother because I thought I had seen some sinister person lurking outside my room, she just told me not to be silly. So I never went to my parents for comfort; never told them when I was frightened or unhappy. I was afraid they would be cross with me and I hated to make them cross. I was always a well-behaved child. I was never cheeky; I never answered my parents back. I suppose this was partly because I was such a quiet, mousey child. I was not really capable of rebellion or disobedience, and also I was afraid of losing my parents' love. I craved love and affection, and I never had as much as I wanted from them.

Looking back, I seem to have been a child who always longed to be loved and was never satisfied with the amount of love I received. I no longer blame my parents for this. I know now that the sort of total, unconditional love that I was seeking is more than any ordinary human being can provide. Only Jesus can love like that, and I thank God that I have found that love at last.

I am not one of those people who can say that their schooldays were the happiest of their lives. My ten years of schooling were sheer unrelieved misery for me. From the day I entered Wix's Lane Infants' School to the day I left Lavender Hill Secondary I hated every minute of it. I welcomed any minor illness that might be an excuse for staying at home. Sometimes I would spend half the night biting the side of my mouth so that it would be swollen in the morning and I could plead illness and stay away from school.

'Concentrate, Maureen!'
'Come out of that daydream, Maureen!'

18

'Maureen, I don't believe you've been listening to a single word I've said!'

I irritated the teachers because I never paid attention to my lessons. I wasn't clever. I found it difficult to concentrate or to remember what I had been taught. School work was always a struggle for me. If I had had more interest in it I might have tried harder, but I made no effort to keep up with the others. When the teachers started talking I just cut myself off and let the words wash over me while I escaped into a world of my own. I almost always came bottom of the class, or nearly bottom, in every subject. Though, extraordinarily, on one occasion I actually came top in algebra. That didn't make me develop more of an interest in algebra, I assumed a mistake had been made, and that still seems the most likely explanation!

My main problem with school wasn't really with the teachers. Although my slowness and failure to concentrate exasperated them, at school as at home I was quiet and well-behaved, and anxious to stay out of trouble. No, my real problem was the other children. They were rough and rude and noisy and I was terrified of them. Children are very cruel. They quickly sense when another child is timid and they make that child a victim. Animals are said to be able to 'smell fear' and it seems to be like that with children too. I was pinched and punched and slapped and subjected to all the little physical tortures that children are expert in. I remember children often used to chant:

> Sticks and stones may break my bones,
> But words can never hurt me!

It wasn't true for me. The physical bullying made me miserable but it was the verbal abuse that hurt me most. I hated the teasing and taunting more than anything.

I used to sit on my own in the shed at playtime and think, 'I wish I had a friend, a nice friend who wouldn't hit me, a friend who wouldn't take the mickey out of me.'. Sometimes I did manage to make friends with another girl, but these friendships never lasted long. When I was at junior school I started trying to buy friends by giving them things. The trouble was I didn't have very much to give away. So I started to steal – usually just little trinkets and sweets from Woolworths. My parents would have been horrified if they had known, but I was never found out. I never kept what I stole, but always gave it away to girls who I wanted to be my friends. Also I used to try gaining friendship by lying. It was the little boy in the next-door garden all over again! I told boastful lies about my parents, my possessions, what I did out of school. I don't think the girls believed me. They must have seen me for what I was: a nonentity. I had no hobbies, no interests, no conversation. I suppose it's not surprising that I had no real friends.

My family never went to church, and I wasn't sent to Sunday School. My parents weren't particularly hostile to religion but it was just something they had no interest in. I knew nothing at all about the Bible, about Jesus or Christianity. I suppose I must have been taught some Bible stories at school, though I don't remember hearing any, but as I never listened to or remembered anything my teachers said, that's hardly surprising. When I was about eleven years old, I had a brief spell of singing in the choir at St Barnabas Church. I don't remember the details of how I got involved with that, and it only lasted for a few weeks. I used to wear the special uniform like the others, and I enjoyed it. It made me feel important. But there was no connection in my mind between singing in the choir and Christianity. I must have heard some sermons at St Barnabas, but they would have washed over me just as my school lessons did. I had no idea of what being a Christian meant, no idea of who

Jesus was. The only thing I knew about religion was that it was boring.

I often wonder now what sort of life I might have had if I had been told at that time that Jesus could give me the love I craved, that he could be that special friend that I was always looking for. But God has his own way of working, and acts in his own good time. I believe he knew me and loved me from the beginning, but it would be many years before I would be ready to understand and return that love.

2: The teenager

'Coming down the Town Hall Saturday, Maureen? It's rock-and-roll night.'

'Right. I'll be there, Diane. Call for you half past seven.'

I suppose I was lucky in that I became a teenager shortly after the idea of teenagers caught on in Britain. Before then adolescents had been thought of as 'in-between' or 'at the awkward age'. Then suddenly in the late 1950s everyone was talking about teenagers. Clothes were designed for us, television programmes aimed at us. And, of course, there was the music.

Rock and roll hit Britain in 1956 with the film *Rock Around the Clock*. It all looks very old-fashioned now but at the time it caused riots. Bill Haley and the Comets were swiftly followed by other American rock stars: Little Richard, Chuck Berry, Buddy Holly, the Everley Brothers and, of course, Elvis Presley. Then we started getting our own home-grown stars: Cliff Richard, Billy Fury, Adam Faith. This was way before the days of The Beatles.

As I entered my teens I started to become a little more 'normal'. I found I could relate to the things that other girls were interested in: pop music, dancing, clothes, boys. I started making one or two friends. They weren't close friends and I never kept a friend for long, but they were girls I could go out dancing with. I started going out regularly to the rock-and-roll dances at Battersea Town Hall when I was thirteen years old.

Being so shy and quiet, I might have been expected to be backward in forming relationships with the opposite sex. But this was not the case. I actually had my first boyfriend when I was only eleven years old. We used to meet on Clapham Common, and just sit holding hands. A lot of boys were attracted to me simply because I was so quiet. A lot of the girls were cheeky and tough, and the boys liked my softness.

Although I had always tried to keep a low profile and not be noticed, once I became aware of boys I became different. I wanted them to notice me; I wanted their attention and admiration. I was pretty and I had a good figure and I dressed with an eye to attracting boys. In the late 1950s the fashion was for tight tops with full skirts and lots of stiff, frilly petticoats, sometimes with hoops in. I wore the tightest tops and the stiffest petticoats, and when the fashion changed to high boots and short, tight skirts, mine were the shortest around.

I flaunted myself and flirted, but underneath was the same timid Maureen who just wanted to be loved. I think I went to such lengths to be attractive to boys because I was craving their affection. I wanted to feel that I was important to someone. I liked kissing and cuddling because it made me feel warm and loved. But I didn't want to go any further than necking. I was scared of sex. My parents had told me nothing and there was little in the way of sex education in school in those days. I remember going on holiday with my parents once and meeting a boy there. We kissed and cuddled, and afterwards I was afraid I might have a baby – just from kissing! That's how naive and ignorant I was. Of course I found out more later from other girls, but though some of them were willing to 'go all the way', I wanted nothing to do with it.

I suppose it was partly because of this that I found it difficult to keep boyfriends. They were attracted by my looks and flirtatious manner and were disappointed when I never gave in to their sexual demands. I must admit that it was probably also my lack of conversation that caused boys to drop me after a couple of dates. Even my first boyfriend on Clapham Common when I was eleven complained to his friend that I was boring and he couldn't get me to say a word.

I left school as soon as I was legally allowed to, at the age of fifteen. I had taken no examinations and had no qualifications, but I was lucky. This was a time of full employment, and also I had a father who could pull a few strings for me. Dad got me a job at the Cumberland Hotel as a hairdresser. I was very excited about taking the job. I had always been fascinated by the hotel and I was thrilled to think that I would become part of that glamorous place. And my interest in fashion made me think that being a hairdresser was the sort of work I would enjoy.

I did enjoy working in a big hotel. Just walking through the entrance door made me feel important. It was exciting, too, seeing the famous people who came into the hotel. I remember seeing Max Wall, Adrienne Posta, and many others. I liked seeing the fashionable women who came to have their hair done, although not all of them were respectable women. The first two clients who come into the salon on my first day at work were a couple of high-class prostitutes. They came often and I was always intrigued by them, curious but shocked at the way they earned their living. Little did I then think that the day would come when I too would join their profession.

Just as when I had started school, my main problem when I started work was getting on with the other girls. I was very shy and nervous to start with. I was frightened to talk to anyone and would sit in the staffroom by myself. Then, when I came out, I was sure they had all been talking about me behind my back. But I did eventually make friends with a girl called Lorraine, and later with a girl called Celia, and I used to go out with them in the evenings or at weekends.

During my mid- to late-teenage years I spent a lot of time going out to the various dancehalls, coffee bars, discos and clubs of London. I often wasn't home until two o'clock in the morning. Looking back to that time now I am surprised that my parents allowed me such freedom. As a mother of teenage boys, I always want to know where my children are and when they will be home. But I can't remember my mother or father ever asking me where I was going, who I was going out with, or telling me that I had to be back at a certain time. Of course, London was a safer place then than it is today. There were dangers, obviously, but you could walk the streets at night and not worry about rapists or muggers then. Also, my parents trusted me. I may have been a typical teenager in some ways, but I was never rebellious, and I still had a good relationship with my parents.

I used to go to the Hammersmith Palais with Lorraine. We would have our hair done and dress ourselves up to the nines. When we got to the Palais, we would sit down and have a drink, while looking over the boys who were there.

'Hey, Maureen, do you fancy that one, the one with the blue suit and the side-burns?'

'He's all right, I suppose.'

'His friend's not bad either. They keep looking at us.'

'Ooh, Lorraine, they're coming over!'

And the boys would dance with us, buy us drinks, chat us up. With any luck, one of them might have a car and give us a lift home. Then Lorraine would stay the night with me and we'd stay up half the night giggling and telling each other what the boys had said, and whether they'd tried anything.

When Celia came to work at the Cumberland I used to go out with her in the evenings, around Soho. We would go to coffee bars and stay drinking coffee until the early hours of the morning, when we would walk home. It was all very exciting for me. Soho has always had a reputation as a red-light district, and we often saw prostitutes standing in doorways and inviting men in. Once we went into a club and found that everyone there seemed to be lying around smoking funny-smelling cigarettes and looking vague and dreamy. Two men approached us and offered us a smoke. 'Come on girls,' they said. 'Have a drag. Enjoy yourselves. Let yourselves go.' I was so innocent that I didn't realise what was going on. I had had no experience of drugs. But luckily, Celia knew what was what and we quickly made our departure. This incident frightened me at the time but it didn't deter me from going to Soho again. Thinking now of the risks and dangers that I innocently exposed myself to as a young girl, I can see how God was looking after me and protecting me from harm.

I went out with quite a few different boys. These relationships never lasted long. The boys were just out for a good time and they didn't take me seriously. But I took every one of them seriously. I was always one to let my heart rule my head. I'm not saying I fell in love with each and every boy I went out with, but I wouldn't go out with a boy unless I really liked him, and then I was terribly hurt and upset if he didn't want to see me again. I would sit at home crying, and hoping for the telephone to ring. When it didn't I would weep to myself, 'I don't understand. Why doesn't he want to see me any more? What's wrong with me?' I know the answer now. As I have said, I might have kept boyfriends for longer if I'd have been willing to go further, but it was also because I was too quiet and no fun to be with.

At last one boy did become serious about me. I met him one night when I went out skating. He came up and started talking to me, and then asked if he could take me home. His name was Mick and he had a motorbike, which I found very exciting. I think Mick really fell in love with me. He took me home to meet his Mum and Dad and I started going to his home often for lunch. He would ride his bike through fog or snow just to see me. But I wasn't in love with Mick. He was a diabetic and had to have insulin injections every day. He was on the fat side too. I wanted to give him up long before I did, but I was sorry for him and didn't have the heart. In the end I phoned him and told him it was over. He cried and pleaded with me, and I felt terrible, but I managed not to give in. I knew I couldn't lead him on any more. I didn't forget Mick easily. I used to lie in bed crying when I thought how I had hurt him. I was tempted to phone and tell him how sorry I was, but I realised that this would only make matters worse.

About a year after that I was sitting in a café with a friend called Janet, when two blokes in a car drove up and asked us if we wanted to go for a drive. We got in and we soon paired off. 'My one' was called Terry. I took a close look at him and I knew straight away that here was someone special; here was the one I had been waiting for. It was really love at first sight. It sounds corny but it really happened, just like in the lovesongs: I looked into Terry's deep blue eyes and my heart started thumping. I had never felt like this before. I longed to be in his arms, but incredibly he didn't try anything at all. He just took me home, but he did ask for my phone number.

I couldn't sleep that night. I kept seeing Terry's face in front of me, kept hearing his voice. If he didn't phone me, I thought I wouldn't be able to bear it. The next day I was glued to the phone. At last it rang and I pounced on it.

'Hello.'
'Hello, is that Maureen?'
'Yes, this is Maureen speaking.'
'Maureen, it's Terry. Can I see you some time?'
'Yes, I'd love to!'

'What would you like to do? Go to the pictures? Go for a drive? Go dancing? What do you fancy doing?'

'Anything, Terry. I don't mind.'

'Well, shall I call for you tomorrow night and we can decide then? OK?'

'OK, Terry, see you then.'

That was the first of many dates. I had never been so happy. Sometimes we would go to the seaside and just lie on the beach and talk. I really loved Terry and he said he loved me. But my bliss was not to last long.

'Maureen,' Terry said one night, 'I've got something to tell you. You know I've applied to go into the army?'

'No, I didn't know,' I said, beginning to feel frightened.

'Well, I'm sure I told you, love. It's what I've always wanted to do. Anyway, they've accepted me. I'm starting next week.'

'Next week! But does that mean you'll be going away?'

'Course it does. I've got to go off to do my training and then – who knows – I could be sent anywhere. Anywhere in the world. I've always wanted to travel.'

'But Terry,' I sobbed, 'what about us? Don't you love me any more? Are you just going to go away and forget me?'

He took me in his arms. 'Don't cry, Maureen love. I'll never forget you. Honest. How could I ever forget you? I'll see you when I come home on leave. And I'll write to you. I promise I'll write. And you must promise to write to me.'

I wasn't very good at writing. I had had few occasions in my life when I had needed to write letters. But as soon as Terry left I sat down to write to him, to tell him how much I loved him and missed him. I waited for the postman every day, hoping to find a letter from Terry. I wrote to him again, begging him to reply. Again I waited, with renewed hope, but no reply came. I wrote several more times and it seemed as though my whole life was concentrated on the morning wait for the postman, the rush to the door, then the tears and disappointment when there was no letter for me. I lost my appetite. I couldn't eat or sleep. I thought of nothing except Terry, reliving the times I had spent in his arms, and longing for him.

At last I realised that Terry was never going to write to me. Despite all his promises, he must have forgotten me. I knew I could never forget him, but I forced myself to start living again. I started going out with friends again, to the cinema or to dances, though my heart wasn't in it.

One night my friend and I had been to see a film at a cinema at Clapham Junction, and then we went on to a café, rather a rough dive. We were sitting drinking tea when a young bloke came in. He joined us and started talking, then he asked if he could see me home. His name was Tony. He kissed me outside our house, but when his hands started to wander I stopped him sharply. He told me afterwards that if I hadn't stopped him then he wouldn't have wanted to see me again. He had no time for girls who were easy.

I started to go out with Tony regularly. We used to meet at Clapham Junction and Tony was always late. We would go to the Railway Arms for a drink, then I would sit there over my drink all evening while Tony played darts. Then he would take me home and come in for a cup of tea. One night we were sitting in our kitchen, kissing, when a mouse ran across the floor. I screamed and jumped onto a chair, expecting Tony to help. But he was standing on a chair too! When my Mum and Dad came in to see what the commotion was about, they burst out laughing to see the pair of us cowering on chairs.

I had to admit that Tony was a weak person. I became fond of him and I knew he was getting fonder and fonder of me, but I couldn't feel about him as I had about Terry. Tony was too much like me really. He was quiet and weak and had no interests. He worked in a fishmonger's and had no ambition. I also found out that he was an epileptic and had fits. I felt very sorry for him. It was just like it had been with Mick, but this time I had got too involved to get out of the relationship. My parents weren't all that keen on Tony, but I went to his home often and I got on well with his family and knew they liked me.

I didn't treat Tony well. If we went to a party I would drink a lot and then spend the evening flirting with other blokes. I still wanted admiration and attention all the time. When I had been with Terry, just his admiration had been enough for me, but when I was with Tony I liked to hear other men praise my good looks and say what a lucky fellow Tony was. I sometimes even went in for a bit of snogging behind Tony's back. It was the same old story. I wanted people to like me. I wanted to feel important. I was still shy underneath but drink gave me false courage and I would mess about and make a fool of myself.

At last Tony asked me to marry him and I accepted him. My parents were not very happy about the engagement. They didn't feel he was the right man for me, and they felt uncomfortable with him. Whenever he was in the house and they came in he would leave. In my heart I too knew that I didn't really love Tony, but I defended him to my parents, and stuck by him.

Then something devastating happened. One Sunday morning, the doorbell rang and I opened it to find Dave, who was a friend of Terry's, standing there.

'Terry's home, Maureen. He wants to see you.'

'Terry! Oh . . . where is he?'

'He's down the pub. Do come and see him, Maureen.'

I didn't know what to do. I was afraid to see Terry, afraid to start up all that hurt again, but Dave persuaded me and I went to the pub. As soon as I saw Terry I knew I still felt the same about him.

'Maureen,' he said, 'I'm back. I had to see you.'

'You never wrote to me,' I whispered.

'I know, Maureen, and I'm sorry. Honestly, I'm so sorry. I can't explain now, but anyway I want to make up for it. Will you come back to me, Maureen?'

'I can't, Terry. I'm engaged.'

'I know. I've heard. But, Maureen, I don't believe you really love this bloke. Break it off with him, please. Marry me, Maureen.'

I felt faint as I saw Terry take a box from his pocket. 'Look, Maureen, I've got the ring and everything. I really mean it. Please, Maureen.'

'I can't,' I said, on the verge of tears. 'I can't do that to Tony. I just can't. Don't ask me to, Terry.'

Terry kept pleading and I just longed to fall into his arms and say yes. But I knew that Tony would be heart-broken if I ended our engagement and I couldn't bear to cause him so much pain. Terry finally said that he would leave me his phone number in case I changed my mind. When he walked out I had to restrain myself from running after him.

That afternoon I met Tony. He noticed that I was very quiet and preoccupied and asked me what was the matter. I didn't answer, but tears filled my eyes. Tony became tearful, too.

'What's the matter, Maureen. Have I done something?'

'No, it's not that, Tony.'

'What is it then? Don't you love me any more? You do still love me, Maureen, don't you? You will marry me?'

'Yes, of course I will. Nothing's the matter. Don't be upset. Don't worry.'

I just didn't have the heart to tell him what had happened. My parents knew and they urged me to give Tony up.

'Maureen, you can't sacrifice your life by marrying Tony if it's Terry you really want,' my Dad said. 'It's not too late to give him up.'

But I was stubborn. I had committed myself to Tony and I couldn't let him down. I was determined to go through with the wedding, and we went ahead with the plans. I persuaded myself that I did love Tony, but my friends weren't taken in. One of them actually said on my wedding day, 'You're marrying Tony out of pity, not love.'

I wasn't excited as a girl on the brink of marriage should be. All I could think of was that I had lost Terry. I even went out with one of Tony's friends behind his back. Nothing seemed to matter to me any more.

I drifted along, making plans for the wedding and for our future together but it all seemed unreal to me. We bought wedding rings; I made decisions about my dress, and bridesmaids; we looked for somewhere to live.

At last the day arrived. I did feel excited the night before, or at least nervous. In the morning I went to the Cumberland and had my hair done and nails manicured. Everyone was coming up to me and asking me how I was feeling. Lorraine and Celia, my friends from the Cumberland, were to be my bridesmaids, and they came back to the house with me for lunch. My father had tears in his eyes as we left for the church. Although he was unhappy with the marriage he had been marvellous, doing all the catering for the wedding and going off in the early morning to buy carnations in the market. A reception had been arranged in the church hall, with 150 guests.

And so at nineteen years of age my single life ended. I became Tony's wife in St Barnabas Church, where I had once sung in the choir.

3: The wife

Tony and I were more fortunate than most young married couples. We had found a lovely flat to rent in a good area of Streatham, and had managed to furnish it completely. My parents had bought us the kitchen furniture and we had bought the rest. We had a kitchen, living room, a 'best room' and one bedroom with french windows opening out onto a large garden. We arrived at the flat after the wedding to a warm welcome from the couple who lived upstairs. We sat on the bed with them and opened some of our presents. Then they left us, and we were alone together.

Here I was, a bride on her wedding night, and my main emotion was one of guilt. My parents had gone to so much trouble over the wedding. Tony loved me so much and we had this lovely place to live. This should have been the happiest day of my life. But I knew already that I had made a terrible mistake. Even during the wedding reception, while everyone was enjoying themselves, I had been fighting back the tears. I couldn't keep Terry out of my thoughts. I couldn't help wishing that it was he that I had married instead of Tony.

We didn't have a honeymoon. We were both back at work after the weekend, and that was probably a good thing, for it was important for me to settle into the new routine of married life as soon as possible. I knew I must make an effort to forget Terry and accept my new role as Tony's wife.

I still had my job at the Cumberland, while Tony worked as a fishmonger in Wardour Street. We used to set off in the morning together and catch the same bus to work, and on Saturdays, after I had finished work at one o'clock, I would meet Tony and we would go home together. There were always chores waiting for me at home. I didn't mind the cooking. I had learned to cook from watching my parents. But I hated ironing. It used to take me half an hour to iron one of Tony's shirts. I wanted to do it properly so he would be pleased, for in those early days I was determined to be a good wife. Tony never helped me with any of the housework. He always seemed to be tired and when he came home from work usually wanted only to watch the television and sleep. He was incapable of making so much as a sandwich or a cup of tea for himself and I had to wait on him hand and foot. I had known he was a weak person, but now I realised the full extent of his incompetence. He could not even tie his own tie or make a telephone call for himself.

Perhaps it was partly Tony's illness that made him so feeble. After we had been married for three weeks he had a fit one night. I had never seen anyone having a fit before and was very frightened. I remembered hearing that there was a danger of epileptics biting their tongues during fits and I tried to put my fingers in Tony's mouth, but he bit me. I was terrified, but eventually I learned how to cope, and also Tony's health improved and the fits became less frequent.

I was lonely at Streatham. Tony and I never talked to each other. My life just seemed to be a cycle of work, chores, and watching Tony sleep on the settee or in front of the television. I sometimes went to have a cup of tea and a chat with Sibyl who lived upstairs, but that seemed to be the full extent of my social life. I missed my Mum and Dad, whom we only saw on Sundays. So, when I heard that there was a flat going near where my parents lived, I was anxious to move. My cousin had just married and moved into the bottom flat in a house in Clapham and the top flat was vacant.

We moved to Clapham but there was little change in our lives. Tony did not become any more helpful or domesticated. He finished work three hours earlier than I did but when I returned home I would invariably find Tony asleep and no preparations made for dinner. He would not even have washed up the breakfast things. The only time we ever did anything together was on Saturday nights when we might go out for a drink or to a party, and even then Tony did not pay me much attention. At that stage I felt it would be wrong to flirt with other men, although I was often tempted.

I was glad to be living closer to my parents, but in some ways it made the situation between me and Tony even worse. Seeing my parents regularly, I could not help comparing Tony with my father, who helped my mother with the cooking, the shopping, and all the household chores. He was so considerate and affectionate and I wished Tony were more like him. Dad used to come to the flat and do the decorating and help with repairs and so on – things that Tony couldn't or wouldn't do. It was a strange situation, looking back on it. I was coming to rely on Dad as a wife would on a husband, while I was having to treat my actual husband more as a child. I always felt that Tony wanted a mother more than a wife. He resented my closeness to my parents and my dependence on my father and was jealous of my relationship with them. He was aware that they did not think much of him as a son-in-law, and there was constant conflict between us over this.

Then, one evening I went to see the doctor because I had missed a couple of periods. When I was told that I was pregnant I was wild with joy. I could hardly believe it. I had always loved babies and had longed to have one of my own. I ran home to tell Tony the good news.

'Tony, Tony, you're going to be a father!'

He looked at me blankly. 'Who, me?'

'Yes, you!' I shouted. His reaction was far too unenthusiastic for my liking and I insisted on going round to my parents that evening to tell them the news. I knew that they would be as excited as me. There were tears of joy in their eyes when I told them. Mum kept turning to Dad and saying, 'You're going to be a grandfather, Jim', and he would reply, 'And you a nan'.

During my pregnancy the contrast between my father and Tony became even more striking. I had sciatica all the way through and was often in pain, but Tony still would not even make the bed or wash up to help me. My parents were disgusted by his laziness and Dad used to meet me from work or help me with my shopping so I would not have to struggle home in pain.

It became clear to us that once the baby arrived we would not be able to manage in a one-bedroom, upstairs flat. Around that time there was an overpopulation problem in London and people were being encouraged to move to smaller towns in the Home Counties. I had an aunt and uncle who had moved to Basingstoke and that gave us the idea of applying for a house there. There was a three-month waiting list so we decided that Tony would go to Basingstoke and find a job and digs for himself. He would stay there during the week and come and see me at weekends. We put our furniture in store and I went back to live with my parents until a house was ready.

I remember crying as I saw Tony off at Victoria. I was sad to think of him going off to a strange place and living all alone in one room. But I soon got used to the situation and, in a way, those few months were the happiest of our marriage. During the week it was just like old times. I was back sleeping in my old bedroom. I continued to work, and I would come home in the evenings and sit with Mum and Dad listening to the wireless or watching television. Absence made me fonder of Tony. I missed him and would look forward to his letters and his weekend visits. Seeing him only at weekends, it was more like our courting days again as we planned our future together. He had found a job as a storeman at an engineering company, and the application for a house was going ahead. I was longing to have the baby and for us all to be together in our new house, but in the meantime I was enjoying being at home and the luxury of being spoiled by my Mum and Dad. They made sure I took it easy, and helped me to buy a pram and baby clothes.

The baby was three weeks overdue before I was taken into hospital to have my labour induced. I was alone during my twelve-hour labour and remember the pain and misery until, at last, just about midnight, Garry was born. I cried for joy when I saw the beautiful, perfect little boy. My cousin Carol rang the hospital so she was the first to hear the news, and she rushed round to my parents' house. It was twelve-thirty and they were asleep, but my father staggered to the door. There stood Carol saying, 'Jim, Maureen's had a boy!' 'Oh, thank you,' yawned my father, then he shut the door, and went back to bed. A few minutes later my mother asked who it was at the door. 'Only Carol to say that Maureen has had a boy,' muttered my father, and then suddenly he woke up. 'A boy! Maureen's had a boy!' They went downstairs for a cup of tea, thrilled to be grandparents at last.

My parents came to the hospital that evening with flowers and cards, but Tony could not visit me until the Friday evening. He looked at his son and said that he would go back and tell the council that he was a father now and press them to get us a house soon so that we could all live together. I was not happy in the hospital. The babies were left by the side of our beds all day and night. It was impossible to get any rest or to sleep at night, and it was often difficult to find a nurse if we had problems. I often did have problems, with this being my first baby. He seemed to cry and be sick more than any of the others. I left hospital exhausted and depressed, and feeling quite unable to cope. It was a good thing that my mother was there to help me.

At last, a letter came from Tony to say that a three-bedroom house was available in South Ham in Basingstoke. My parents took me down to see it and I loved it, so we arranged to move in as soon as possible. I was sad to leave my parents but excited about having our own home.

At first I was happy, just having a decent size house with our own garden. But I missed my Mum and Dad and I felt terribly lonely. I had worked right up until my last month of pregnancy and I was not used to being alone in a house all day. I had dreamed of the joys of looking after a baby, but I found that the reality was very different. Garry continued to be crotchety, not sleeping and forever crying and being sick. I felt frightened of the responsibility of caring for him, and I'm sure my anxiety and lack of confidence got through to him and made him even more difficult. I used to sit in the house all day crying. I was in a strange town, with no friends, and I felt completely lost and alone, with no one to turn to. Tony gave me no help with the baby. He never bathed him or fed him or changed a nappy. His only concern was that his sleep was not to be disturbed, and he did not seem to understand that I was at the end of my tether.

I had never been any good at making friends, but it had mattered less when I had my parents near and a job to go to. Now I used to watch other young mums pushing their prams and chatting to each other and I would long for a friend. I used to watch my next-door neighbour over the fence. She seemed friendly and pleasant but I hardly spoke to her because I could never think of anything to say. She and her husband and their little boy seemed so happy and self-contained. I watched them from my window going out for walks together, and I envied her, for Tony had no interest in our going out together as a family.

One day there was a knock at the door and I opened it to find Barbara, my next-door neighbour, standing there. 'Maureen, are you all right?' she asked. 'I wondered if you needed help.' I just broke down on the spot. Barbara, who barely knew me, seemed to have realised what my own husband could not comprehend – that I was sinking into a deep depression and desperately needed help. I told Barbara how difficult I found it coping with Garry, and she was so kind and understanding, and offered to look after Garry whenever I felt I could not cope.

It was a help having Barbara to take Garry off my hands from time to time, although I was still lonely and depressed. But now my life was to change again, for my parents decided to move to Basingstoke, and Tony and I made the decision to move to Winklebury Estate, which was where my aunt and uncle lived, and where we would be nearer to my parents.

Once we moved to Winklebury, I was less lonely. I saw quite a lot of my Mum and Dad but I still felt, as I had when I was a child, that they were wrapped up in each other, had their own lives to lead, and would not want me constantly around them. Probably I was being unfair to them, thinking like that, for they always seemed pleased to see me and made me welcome. It was certainly a relief to know that they were near and would be on hand if I ever needed them.

There was quite a lively social life available on the estate. There was a working man's club and people often gave parties, and Tony and I started going out regularly on Saturday evenings, getting a young girl in to babysit. As ever, Tony paid me little attention on these occasions, and now I did start flirting again, wearing short skirts and doing all I could to attract other men. I wasn't really interested in being unfaithful to Tony, but I was looking for the fun and the attention that Tony could not give me. Because I never felt really loved and wanted by Tony, and was not even wholly confident of my parents' love, I was ready to be taken in by any man who showed me kindness or admiration.

A girl called Julie moved into our block. Her marriage was on the rocks, her husband was having an affair, and she was anxious to be friends with me. We started going out in the evenings together, going for a drink and chatting up men. It was harmless enough fun, like being single again, but in the end Julie returned to Plymouth, where her family lived, and my social life was limited by my second pregnancy.

From the start, Graham was easier than Garry had been. It was an easy birth, Graham was a less troublesome baby and I coped much better with him. Tony was still no help at all, but now I had my parents near. It was much as it had been in London, with my father doing all our decorating and my parents – rather than Tony – worrying about my welfare. Tony never seemed concerned to see me struggling with two small children and bags of shopping. He couldn't be bothered to come shopping with us at weekends like other fathers. He never took his children out, but I would walk over to my parents and they would take the boys out. Dad was more like a father to the boys than Tony was. It was he who took them out, played with them, bought them presents. Again Tony became jealous of my father and we quarrelled over this.

Things were far from ideal, but I might have settled down to my life had it not, at this time, dealt me a dreadful blow from which I was unable to recover. One dark January evening there was a knock at the door and I opened it to find two policemen standing outside.

'Mrs Brown?'

'Yes, what is it? Come in.'

'We'd like you to come with us, Mrs Brown. I'm afraid we have bad news for you. Your father is dead. He committed suicide.'

I followed them to the car in a daze, unable to take in what they were telling me. They drove me to my mother's house where I found my mother and aunt, both in tears. I rushed into my mother's arms, but she was too distraught to explain anything. Eventually we sat down and my aunt told me what had happened. My father had had a hospital appointment as he had been feeling unwell recently and had been losing weight. But he didn't go to the hospital. My mother had returned from work to find the house in darkness. She smelled gas and went into the kitchen where my father was lying over the gas stove with a blanket over his head.

I just couldn't believe it and neither could my mother. Dad had so much to live for. He was only fifty-four. He and my mother loved each other and they had been happy in Basingstoke. They had booked a holiday and were buying a new car. The only explanation that seemed possible was that my father had become obsessed with his health problem. He was rarely ill and panicked at the thought of illness. My mother was sure that he had become convinced that his symptoms were caused by cancer and that he wanted to die before he became a burden to his family.

Because of the circumstances of my father's death there had to be an autopsy. When they examined his body they found there was no trace of cancer. There was nothing wrong with him at all. If only Dad had gone to the hospital and had tests they could have reassured him that there was nothing wrong. I understand now that the devil uses our fear to work for evil in our lives.

I tried to comfort my mother but with little success. I wished that I could stay with her but it didn't seem possible. Tony was not capable of looking after the boys and I couldn't bring them to my mother's as she wouldn't want to cope with small children when she was feeling so low. As for myself, for a while I was still stunned and my emotions were numb. I didn't even cry. But after a few weeks I became very depressed. I saw the doctor who told me that I was having a late reaction to the shock of my father's death. The pills I was given were no help. I had been unable to cry but now I was unable to stop crying. I felt as though I had lost everything and life didn't seem worth living. I still had my mother, my husband and my children, but the most important person in my life had gone.

Tony was no comfort to me at this time. He had always been jealous of Dad and I suppose my heartbroken grief was further proof that I had loved my father more than I loved him. He wouldn't come with me to visit my mother and he wouldn't look after the boys when I went, so it was difficult for me to see her, much as I wanted to. When she came to us there was always tension. Tony barely spoke to her and she was upset to see the way he left all the work to me and expected to be waited on.

Eventually I began to emerge from my depression and I started to go out again on Saturday nights. But my father's death had changed me. Tony's inadequacies had already been driving me to seek admiration and warmth from other men, but now this became less a matter of wanting fun than a desperate need for love. I felt so empty and lost with my father gone. I had sometimes doubted his love but now I remembered all the affection he had shown in his kindness and consideration towards me and I felt that I had lost the one person who had loved and wanted me.

Tony was now working nights and I saw almost nothing of him. He came in at seven-thirty in the morning and went straight to bed and slept until about four-thirty. Then he left for work again at six p.m. Even at weekends there was no companionship between us.

When Tony wasn't sleeping or watching television he was out drinking at the club without me. He never wanted to come out with me and the boys, so I used to take them out to my Mum's and leave him at home. My Mum was pleased to see us. She was still lonely though she was coping and had a lot of support from her family. We did become a little closer at this time although I still found it very difficult to have a conversation with her.

I started going out without Tony. It was really just a matter of time before I met another man – anyone who showed me a little affection and warmth would have done. Les was a housepainter, married with a family. He was kind and attentive to me and made it clear how much he wanted me. With Tony working nights it was easy to have Les round after the boys had gone to sleep, and I began an affair with him. I found him easier to talk to than Tony; he used to buy me presents and seemed really fond of me, and I persuaded myself that I loved him.

Then Les moved to London and we were unable to meet often. We agreed that I would go to London with the boys for a week, staying with an aunt, so that we could meet every night. Tony was not very pleased about our going but he saw us off on the coach and I soon had the boys settled in with my aunt. I met Les every night that week. He offered to leave his wife for me but I said no. I didn't want to break up Les's family. When Tony met us from the coach and asked about our week I found it difficult to lie to him, though I knew I must. I didn't want to hurt him and anyway I was pretty sure that this week had marked the end of my affair with Les.

Although I was no longer seeing Les I continued to go out a lot and I felt that my confidence was boosted. All the men I met seemed to be attracted to me and I was constantly being pestered to sleep with them. I started seeing a lot of an old friend from London whose hus-band, Chris, had always made it obvious that he fancied me. I enjoyed the attention and began to feel that I was important at last. I should say that, in all this, I never neglected my boys. In fact my increased confidence meant that I felt more able to cope with life in general, and that included bringing up my children. Garry and Graham were now three and one, lively boys full of fun and mischief. I took them out often, read to them and played with them and made sure they were never short of love and attention from me.

One night when Tony was working and the boys were in bed I was sitting watching television when there was a knock at the door. Les was outside.

'Hello, Maureen,' he said. 'I've come down from London just to see you.'

'Go away,' I said. I had almost forgotten Les and I didn't want to see him. But he put his foot in the door and I was forced to ask him in. He told me he was working at Basingstoke for a week. We talked and then he began fondling me. I rejected him and he lost his temper, raising a hand to strike me. I started crying, terrified that he might beat me up, that the children would wake, and that Tony would hear about it. Les calmed down and apologised.

'I'm sorry, Maureen. I've just been waiting for this so long. I know now that I love you. I want to be with you always.'

I didn't know what to say. I didn't really want Les but his gentle words won me over and I responded to his kisses. At last I persuaded him to go as it was late, and I went to bed to spend a sleepless night. Even Tony noticed in the morning that I was upset, but I just told him that I had had a bad night. I was restless all day, afraid to go out in case I saw Les but nervous that he might actually come to the house while Tony was there.

Les did not come but Chris, my friend's husband, turned up. He sat down to chat and the boys were all over him straight away, wanting him to play with them. Whenever anyone came to the house they were like that because Tony so rarely played with them. After a while Chris started telling me that he loved me. Not long before I had welcomed having different men all making up to me, but now I felt so confused and upset that I just didn't want to hear it.

'Stop it, Chris,' I said. 'I don't want you to go on with this. I love Tony and I love my boys and I don't want anyone to get hurt.'

Chris looked at me. 'I loved you even back when we were in London,' he said. I remembered that it had been Chris who had told me I was marrying Tony out of pity. He had always known how shallow my love for Tony was.

'I'm sorry,' I told Chris, 'but I just don't want to hear any more.'

'All right, Maureen,' he said, 'but remember what I've said. I really mean it. I do love you and I'll always be around and waiting in case you change your mind.'

Chris left then, leaving me in a turmoil. I knew I did not love either him or Les and I felt like running away from the whole situation. I began to wonder about getting a part-time job. It would give me more independence, get me out of the house, and give me something else to think about. I saw an advertisement for a cleaning job at the local infant's school and asked Tony how he felt about my applying for it.

'I'm bored at home all day,' I told him.

'Yes, but who's going to look after the boys?' he asked.

'I'd just be working for an hour or so in the afternoon,' I told him. 'It would only mean your getting up at four and looking after them until I got home at five-thirty.'

Tony wasn't keen but eventually he agreed and the next morning I took the boys and went along to the school and asked if the job was still available. I was told that it was and that I should come for an interview at four-thirty. As I walked home I noticed Les working on a scaffold. I felt my heart pounding with fear. I pretended not to see him and hoped that he had not seen me.

I woke Tony at four, left the boys with him, and went off for my interview. The first person I saw when I went into the school was a tall man wearing a blue velvet jacket, a bow tie and pin-striped trousers. He looked very impressive and I wondered if he was the headmaster. I went to the office and was taken to see the head, who was not the man I had seen. It was a very brief interview and I was told at the end that I had the job and could start the next day. The secretary showed me out of the office, saying, 'Before you go, I'll introduce you to our caretaker. He will be able to show you what you have to do and where everything is kept.' And she led me to the man in the blue velvet jacket! 'This is our caretaker, Ron Sims. Ron, this is Maureen Brown who is going to start work here as a cleaner tomorrow. Can you show her where everything is, please.'

Ron started showing me where all the cleaning equipment was kept and explaining the work but I was barely listening. I was absolutely bowled over by this man! He was big and muscular and very masculine and rugged looking yet with a sensitivity about his eyes and mouth that made me feel weak at the knees. As he talked I felt my heart thumping and I couldn't take my eyes off him. In the end, he said, 'Well, goodbye love, see you tomorrow. I'm really looking forward to working with you.' He showed me out but halfway down the path I turned back and saw Ron still standing by the door looking at me.

When I got home Tony was waiting for me to cook his dinner. He ate it and then went off to work. He didn't ask about the interview and I didn't tell him. That night Les turned up. 'Why did you pretend not to see me up on the scaffold this afternoon?' he asked. 'And what were you doing coming out of the school?'

'I didn't see you, Les,' I lied, trying to ignore his suspicious expression. 'I was at the school for an interview.

I've got a job as a cleaner there, starting tomorrow. That's good, isn't it?'

Les wasn't interested in my job. He started asking me to go away with him and I told him again that I intended staying with Tony and that I wasn't prepared to break up two families. I felt frightened and restless and I just didn't want this involvement any more. Les didn't seem to understand how I felt and started to make advances to me, but I pretended that Tony would be returning soon, and managed to get rid of him.

I couldn't get to sleep that night. Every time I heard a noise I was afraid that Les had come back and would discover that I had lied about Tony coming home that night. I was afraid of Tony finding out about Les. I was afraid that my mother too would find out. I was worried that the boys would be hurt. And there was something else keeping me awake. Every time I closed my eyes I pictured a tall man in a velvet jacket looking at me as I walked down the school path.

When Tony came home the next morning he remembered to ask me if I had got the job.

'Yes, I start today at four.'

'Oh, that means I'll have to get up early,' he grunted. 'I'd better go straight to bed now.'

I managed to get through my chores that day although I felt nervous and jumpy. At about three-thirty I started to get ready to go out. I found myself taking extra trouble with my hair and make-up. I changed into a light jumper and a miniskirt as though I was preparing for an evening out, rather than going to clean out toilets and classrooms. I told myself I was just feeling nervous because of the trouble with Les, and that I was excited because I was starting a new job. But I knew the real reason for the excitement, the nerves and the care with my appearance. I just couldn't wait to see Ron Sims again!

4: Ron

By the time I had been working at the school for a week I was already hopelessly in love with Ron Sims. Every time he spoke to me I felt weak. I lived for four o'clock when I could go into work and see him. I was fairly sure that he was attracted to me. He was always making excuses to come and see how I was getting on, and then staying to chat. There were three other cleaners, and the four of us and Ron got together for a tea break every afternoon. I found that whenever I looked at Ron he was looking at me, and I felt that unspoken messages were passing between us every time our eyes met. Sometimes during the day I would go out shopping so that I would pass the school, hoping that I might see Ron; usually he would be looking out for me and would come out so that we could chat.

Gradually I started to get to know Ron and to find out something about his past. He told me that he had been married and had four children, that his wife had treated him badly and left him, and that she would not let him see the children. He confided in me that he missed his children badly and that he was deeply hurt by his wife's behaviour. I felt very sorry for him and longed to comfort him, but this was not the sort of pity that I had felt for Tony. No two men could have been more different. Ron was so confident, masculine, strong and extrovert, and his vulnerability on this one issue just made him appear more lovable to me.

I had never met a man like Ron before. He had a reputation as a playboy and there was certainly something of that about him, for he dressed flamboyantly and drove a large American-type car. He was a man who got on well with women and knew how to talk to them; when he spoke to me he made me feel that I was really important to him.

For weeks I could think of nothing but Ron. I fell deeper and deeper in love and I knew he had become fond of me too. Our snatched meetings at work were exciting but they no longer satisfied me. I dreamed about spending an entire evening with Ron, and finally I decided to do something about it. Normally I would always have waited for the man to make the first move, but now love had made me uncharacteristically bold. I approached Ron one day before I left work and said, 'You know Tony is working on nights. He leaves at six. Why don't you come round tonight?'

Ron looked thoughtful. 'Well,' he began, 'I don't know . . .'

'Oh, please come, Ron,' I begged. 'We'd be able to talk. You know we can't talk properly here.'

'All right them, I'll be there at eight.'

I gave him a quick peck on the cheek and ran before he could change his mind. I felt almost sick with excitement and joy. At last I was going to be alone with Ron! I went home and tried to act normally in front of Tony and the boys, but I was aware of the butterflies in my stomach and the thumping of my heart. Tony left and I hurried the boys off to bed, then took a long leisurely bath and set to work making myself up and dressing to kill. I was just applying a final coat of lipstick when I heard a knock at the door. I looked at my watch. Only seven-thirty. Ron must have decided to come early. I flew downstairs and opened the door. There stood Les.

The welcoming smile died on my lips. It was weeks since I had seen or heard from Les, and I had assumed that he had accepted that all was over between us and given up. He was certainly the last person I wanted to see at the moment.

'Surprised?' he asked, with a smirk. I didn't answer, but just stood there helplessly, thinking that Ron might turn up at any minute and hoping I could get rid of Les before they met.

'Well, aren't you going to ask me in?' Les asked, and then I smelled drink on his breath.

'No, I'm not,' I said. 'Please go away. I didn't think you'd be coming any more. I'm sorry, but it's over.'

Les scowled, 'What do you mean it's over?'

'I've met someone else,' I said, 'someone I really love.'

It was the wrong thing to have said. Les was furious. His face darkened. 'You slut!' he shouted, and I thought he was going to hit me. I tried to close the door but his foot was in it.

'Please go,' I sobbed. 'I'm sorry . . . please go . . .'. I was frightened that Les would force his way into the house, frightened that Ron would arrive while he was there. Suddenly Les stumbled slightly, enough to make his foot slip from the doorway. I seized the opportunity and slammed the door shut. Les immediately started banging at the door and shouting, while I cowered inside, crying. At last the commotion stopped and, after a moment or two, I peeped through the window to check that Les had really gone. I couldn't see anyone outside but, as I looked, I saw Ron approaching the house. As he reached the door I opened it a crack, fearful that Les might still be lurking, and whispered to Ron, 'Come in, quick.'

This was hardly the right start to the romantic evening I had dreamed of for so long. I was still shaking with fear, my face was damp with tears, my careful make-up spoiled. Of course Ron saw immediately that something was very wrong.

'What's up, love?' he asked. 'What's upset you?'

'This man was here . . . I was frightened . . .'

'What man? Tell me all about it,' Ron said, and so I found myself explaining about Les. As I talked I saw

Ron's face hardening, and as I finished he turned from me.

'I might as well go now,' he said harshly.

I was devastated. 'Why? Why, Ron? Please don't go.'

'I thought you were different,' he said. 'I've had enough of women who go from one affair to another. I was hurt enough by my wife and I'm not going to get involved with another woman like that.'

I burst into tears. I felt that my heart would break if Ron walked out on me now. Abandoning all pride, I clung to him and begged him to stay. 'I'm not like that, Ron. Honestly, please believe me. No one else means anything to me. I love you,' I wept.

Ron was quiet for a minute, and then gave me a hug and said, 'All right, I'll stay.' Once he had relented he behaved as though nothing had happened and my tears soon dried as he opened a large carrier bag he had brought in with him and presented me with a pot of flowers. He then delved into the bag and, to my amazement, produced a large piece of steak, some vegetables, a bottle of wine and a couple of candles.

'Sit down,' he said, 'I'm going to cook us a meal.' He sauntered into my kitchen as though it were his own and I watched, hardly able to believe my eyes, as he calmly and confidently grilled the steak, fried chips, cooked peas and tomatoes. When he had finished he opened the wine, lit the candles, set two places at the table, and we began to eat. The meal was perfectly cooked but I was hardly able to appreciate it properly, for my emotions had endured such a battering. First the upset with Les; then the despair when it looked as though I would lose Ron; now the wonder of being waited on by this amazing man. I had never known anything like this before. For years I had waited on Tony and no man had ever cooked me a meal before, except for my father, of course, who was a professional cook.

When we had finished eating Ron took my hand and led me to the front room, and we sank down in front of the fire in each other's arms. I felt as though I was in the middle of a wonderful dream, and my only fear was that I would wake up. I was so much in love, and I knew now that I wanted to be with Ron always and I would do anything to bring that about.

'Hey, Maureen, come in here a minute.' I had just arrived at work and Ron had been waiting for me. He ushered me into an empty classroom and closed the door.

'You'll never guess what I've been doing,' he said. There was a triumphant gleam in his eye.

'What have you been up to?'

'I've found somewhere for us to live. You and me, Maureen. It's only a caravan but it would be somewhere for us to be together.'

I was speechless. Ron mistook my silence for reluctance and continued in coaxing tones, 'Please, Maureen. Please come away with me. I do love you.'

I threw my arms round him. 'Of course I will. All I want is to be with you forever.' Then I hesitated. 'But Ron, what about my children? I can't leave my boys.'

'Bring them with you.'

'Are you sure, Ron? Are you sure you want them?'

'I'll treat them as though they were my own,' Ron declared. 'They're part of you and anything of yours is mine now.'

Ron started telling me about the caravan, which was on a site in Hook, a village on the M3 about six miles away. I was too happy and too stunned by this new turn of events to listen to all the details. We agreed that I would have the boys ready at seven o'clock that evening and Ron would pick up the three of us and all our luggage.

I spent the rest of the afternoon at work in a daze, my happiness marred only by the constant nagging thought: how am I going to break the news to Tony? I knew it would be a dreadful blow to him and would come completely out of the blue. Although he didn't show me much affection I knew he loved me in his way, and he was so dependent on me to look after him. With my father's death still haunting me, my main fear was that Tony might be driven to suicide.

As soon as I got home and saw Tony I realised that I wasn't going to have the courage to tell him face to face. I would have to leave a note for him. When he left for work I started to pack and get the boys ready. Then I wrote to Tony explaining what I was doing. I finished it: 'Please don't do anything silly. Find someone else. I'm sorry. Maureen.'

I didn't have time to get jumpy for Ron was early, and packing the car with all our things was tricky. In the end we realised that there just wasn't room for all the luggage and three passengers, so Ron said he would take the luggage and then come back for us. Now I did start to get nervous. Ron seemed to be away for so long, and the children were getting very excited. They didn't really understand what was happening but they knew they were going to ride in Ron's big car. Just as I was telling myself that he had taken all our things and was never coming back, I heard the car draw up outside. I got the boys into the back of the car and then followed them. I closed my front door for the last time and did not look back as we drove away.

5: On the site

It was dark when we arrived at Hook. I couldn't make out much of the site or see the outside of the caravan properly. We stepped inside and Ron put down our bags and cases and looked at me.

'Happy, love?'

'Yes. I'm happy to be with you.' It was blissful to be in Ron's arms and to know we were together for always. As I unpacked and got the boys to bed I took in the layout of our new home. It was a twenty-two foot caravan. At one end was a small bedroom where the boys would be sleeping. This was divided by two doors from the main part of the caravan, which contained the living quarters with beds which pulled out from the wall, and a tiny kitchen with a sink, a calor gas stove and a bench which served as a dining table. There was no running water inside the caravan and the toilets were a short walk away. It was very cramped for four people, and anything but luxurious, but I was not complaining. I was with Ron and nothing else mattered.

Ron cooked some supper and then we went to bed. We stayed awake for hours, making love and talking. Towards morning Ron fell asleep. I looked at him sleeping next to me and felt a strange sense of unreality. I was more in love than ever and unable to look at Ron without my heart beating faster. Yet I was still astounded that I had actually taken such a huge step, and I could not help brooding about what Tony would do when he read my note.

The boys woke early and I went to fetch water so I could wash them. When I opened the caravan door and saw the site by daylight I could hardly believe my eyes. What a dump this was! It was sordid and derelict. The caravans looked tatty and uncared for, many of them with scruffy, torn curtains at the windows. There were old washing machines and piles of rubbish everywhere. But it was my new neighbours that I found most alarming. I saw a couple of tough-looking, unshaven men in dirty boots and donkey jackets; I saw sluttish women in dressing gowns; all the talk I overheard seemed to be swearwords. I was frightened. This wasn't the sort of thing I was used to. I didn't want to tell Ron how I felt – this was the place he had found for us and no doubt it was the best he could do. But when I returned to the caravan Ron saw that I was shaken by what I had seen. He put his arms round me and said, 'I'll look after you, love.' In the warmth of his strong arms I felt secure and cared for as I had never felt before, and my fears and qualms dissolved. The rest of the day became a holiday. After breakfast Ron drove us to the coast and the boys ran about on the beach while Ron and I sat like a couple of lovebirds.

The honeymoon period did not last long. I began to realise that there was a side of Ron that I had not known about. The other people on the site were a disreputable lot. Few of the couples were married and there were many single mothers. There were drug addicts there, alcoholics, prostitutes, and many people seemed either to have been in prison or to have some connection with the criminal world. The police were often on the site. This was all strange to me but Ron fitted in with no difficulty, in fact it turned out that he already knew some of these people quite well. I knew he had had some brush with the law in the past and was still seeing a probation officer, but he had played this down and I had not been bothered about it. But now I found out that Ron had been in prison more than once, and that his life had been dominated by crime and violence.

As the days passed and Ron mixed more with the people on the site I saw a change in him. The sensitive loving man that I had taken him for was now less often in evidence. I had admired his toughness and masculinity but now that revealed itself as coarseness and swagger. He no longer watched his language while he was with me and he often lost his temper and became abusive and even violent with me. We both gave up our jobs at the school. I stayed on the site all day looking after the boys, but Ron got a job as a ganger on the M3, which was where most of the men on the site worked. He now became virtually indistinguishable in his manner from the other men and I was often frightened of him, though I was still as much in love with him as ever.

Probably I would never have gone away with Ron if I had known about his criminal past, or had been shown the dark side of his personality. I had wanted a man like my father, who would be kind and considerate and take care of me, and Ron had seemed to be just such a man. Over the dark years that were to follow, I rarely saw a glimpse of the man I had taken Ron to be, and it looked as though I had again made a terrible mistake. But the Lord had been guiding me after all. He alone knew Ron's potential; he knew the man that he would become one day, and he knew that Ron was the right man for me.

A couple of weeks after our move to Hook my mother turned up. I didn't know how she had found out where I was, and I was both glad and alarmed to see her. As soon as she appeared, the boys rushed to her and started telling her all about the caravan, and she was obviously reassured to see them looking well and happy. I made her a cup of tea and we sat down to talk.

'Why didn't you tell me you were going and where?' she asked.

'Because you would have tried to stop me and I know I would have given in,' I said.

'Well, maybe I would have,' Mum said. 'But Maureen, why did you do it?'

'I love Ron, Mum. I love him and he loves me and I can't be happy unless I'm with him. Anyway, do you know if Tony is all right?'

'Well, I don't see much of him but I know he's taking it hard. He is seeing a girl called Linda, but I know he's still looking for you. He wants to see the boys.'

'You can tell him where we are if you want,' I said, and just then Ron came in. He was obviously shocked to see my mother but he quickly recovered and turned on the charm. 'So you've found us,' he said. 'I'm so sorry if you've been worried. I promise I'll look after them all.'

The children came in from outside where they had been playing and ran up to Ron and we all had tea together like a happy family. I felt that my mother had accepted Ron. After all, she had never been happy with Tony as a son-in-law and Ron had so much more of a way about him. He kissed her on the cheek when she was ready to leave and promised again to look after us. Mum seemed quite happy and said, 'You know where I am, and you're both very welcome.' Then Ron ran her home in the car and I felt that at least there was one load off my mind.

Our next visitor was less welcome. We had been to the coast one Sunday and shortly after our return there was a knock at the door. When I opened it and saw Tony I felt sick. 'What do you want?' I whispered.

'I want to talk to you. Can I come in?'

'Wait a minute,' I said, and went back inside the caravan. 'Tony's outside,' I told Ron. 'He says he wants to talk to me. What shall I do?'

'Tell him to come in,' Ron said. 'I'll take the boys for a walk while you talk to him.'

I asked Tony in and as soon as Garry saw him, he said, 'Hello Dad,' but Graham had already forgotten him and clung to Ron. Ron took the boys off and Tony and I settled down to talk, but as ever we were unable really to communicate. Tony just kept asking, 'Why? Why?'. I tried to explain that I didn't have any life with him, he didn't take enough interest in me or the boys, we never went out as a family, and that I had been unhappy for a long time.

'Please come back, Maureen,' Tony begged. 'I still love you. I'll change if you come back, I promise. You'll see, everything will be different. Please, Maureen.'

I felt sorry for him but I wasn't going to give in. 'I'm not going to walk out on Ron. He's been hurt by a woman before and I'm not having him hurt again. I'm sorry, Tony, but I love Ron. I'll never leave him.'

We went round in circles with Tony begging me over and over again to return to him, and me repeating that I wouldn't. Eventually I stopped even pitying Tony and felt impatient and irritated with him. I was just longing for him to go. When Ron and the boys came back, Tony turned to Ron and said, 'I'd like to talk, please. Would you come down to the pub with me?'

Ron turned to me and said, 'Is that all right with you?'

'Sure,' I said. 'You go along.'

I waited for Ron's return with mixed emotions. I had felt embarrassed and ashamed of Tony, seeing him with Ron. The last thing I wanted was for Tony to pick a fight – it was obvious that he wouldn't stand a chance against Ron – but he had been so timid and meek in his manner that he seemed like a child next to Ron. I was almost afraid that I would sink in Ron's opinion for having married such a weak, pathetic creature. But a more serious worry arose when Garry kept asking, 'Where's Daddy gone? When will he be back?' and I realised that he had been more affected by leaving his father than I had thought. He wouldn't eat any tea, said he was tired, but didn't sleep when I put him to bed. A voice in my head started whispering, 'Go back to Tony. He is the boys' father. Look how upset Garry is. Go back for his sake.' But I dismissed these thoughts. I knew that I could never be happy if I left Ron to return to Tony, and I told myself that we had seen the last of Tony and that Garry would soon forget him.

We had not seen the last of Tony. When Ron came back he told me that Tony wanted to see the boys occasionally on a Sunday and that he had said that he could, for he was, after all, entitled to as their father. Ron had obviously been upset by the whole business. There were tears in his eyes when he hugged me and said, 'You won't go back to him, will you? You won't leave me?' I tried to reassure him that I loved him and wouldn't leave him, but it was hard to convince him. That night we laid in bed talking and Ron told me how much he still missed his children and how he was still hurt by the way his wife had treated him. He told me things he had not told me before, about his childhood when his mother abused him and showed him no love, and then about his traumatic marriage and how often his wife had left him for other men, and had finally taken the children, though she had cared so little for them. I could understand how he had become distrustful of women and I felt really broken up to see this tough man so vulnerable. We both wept and clung to each other as I told him over and over again that he could trust me, that I loved him, and would not leave him.

We were all unsettled after Tony's visit. Ron was quiet and moody for days, and seemed to have little time for the boys or even for me. Garry was very restless and he began to live for the Sundays when Tony took him and Graham out. Unfortunately, Tony was unreliable, and on some Sundays when he had promised to come he failed to appear. It was heartbreaking for me to see Garry looking out of the window for hours, saying, 'When is Daddy coming?' but it seemed to get on Ron's nerves and eventually he would get up and take Garry out for a walk to settle him down. I told Tony to stop messing the boys about as it was upsetting Garry so much. I felt Tony was only keeping this link with the boys in the

59

hope that I would relent at last and go back to him. Since Tony had appeared back on the scene Garry had stopped accepting Ron, and though Ron treated both the boys well he could not help being affected by Garry's rejection of him.

Although I was now living with the man that I loved, my days started to take on some resemblance to my early married life. Ron seemed to be drifting away from me, and I become very depressed and unable to cope. I would sit for hours crying by myself in the caravan. Each day, as the time for Ron's return from work approached, I would peer nervously through the window, afraid that this would be the day when he wouldn't come back to me. I found it difficult to make friends with the other women on the site, although I did get to know one or two quite well. Most of them seemed to me as tough and alarming as the men.

When I found I was pregnant again things briefly improved. Ron was as excited as I was and this drew us closer together for a while. But he still had bouts of violent and aggressive behaviour that terrified me. I knew that this was partly because he was working very long hours on the motorway and the pressure of work often made him explode when he got home, and I bore the brunt of his tiredness and frustration. When he had reduced me to tears with his abuse he would usually apologise and take me in his arms to comfort me, and I would momentarily recognise the gentle affectionate man I had fallen in love with.

One morning, when I was four months pregnant, Garry woke and was violently sick and obviously feverish. I called the doctor who told me to give him liquids only, but he was unable to keep even those down, so I asked the doctor to look at him again. He arranged for Garry to be taken into hospital in Basingstoke. There they diagnosed salmonella food poisoning and transferred him to Winchester Isolation Hospital. Two days later Graham came down with it too and was taken straight to Winchester.

I visited the boys in hospital every day. I had to take a bus to Basingstoke, then a train to Winchester, and another bus from the station to the hospital. I was not allowed to touch the boys or even get close to them, as they were in isolation. I could only look at them through the door and hope that they were comforted by seeing me there. I used to come home in the evening totally exhausted, both physically and emotionally, and then would often have to face Ron in an aggressive mood. I longed only to sleep but Ron was demanding and inconsiderate and I gave in to him because I was afraid of his anger.

One day, before visiting the hospital, I went into a store in Winchester to buy a couple of little toys for the children. When I got to the cash desk I found I had only one of the two toys I had picked up and, being in a hurry, I thought I would leave it at that and just buy the one. I had to return to the cash desk, though, as I found I had been given too much change. I finally left the shop but, as I walked out, I found myself gently but firmly taken by the arm.

'Excuse me, madam, please could you come back into the store with me.'

'Why? What's the matter? Who are you?'

'I am the store detective. Now, if you would just follow me to the manager's office. . .'

I was taken to the office, my bag was searched, and the other toy was found in it. I protested that I had no idea how it had got there, but they obviously didn't believe me and called the police who took me to the police station. There I went through the humiliating rituals of questioning, fingerprinting, and having my photo taken, before I was officially charged with shoplifting. I couldn't believe that this was happening to me. What would Ron say? Would I be sent to prison? What would happen to my boys? By the time they had finished with me I was distraught and a kind policewoman, seeing my distress and hearing that I had been on the way to visit my children, offered to drive me to the hospital.

When I reached the hospital I was in a state of collapse. The nurse on the children's ward took me into a small room and gave me a cup of tea so that I could compose myself before I saw the boys. As I looked at my children in their net-covered cots, I felt as though my whole world was collapsing. When I eventually arrived home I had to tell Ron what had happened. I had hoped for comfort but received only abuse.

The boys were sent home just before Christmas but, though I had been longing for their return, I found it very difficult to cope with them in my run-down and depressed state. One evening a policeman came to serve me with a subpoena to appear in court, and that night I had a miscarriage. When I finally stood before the magistrate I was in a state of near collapse from the misery and pain of losing the baby, and the ordeal of the court appearance. I was given a conditional discharge, so none of my worst fears were realised, but the shame of the incident lived with me for long after.

The relationship between me and Ron continued to be fraught, and it now seemed as though it was Garry who was causing much of the tension. He had become very disturbed, kept asking for his dad, and would not accept Ron. I tried to persuade Garry to behave decently to Ron but when Ron complained about Garry I was forced into defending my son. Whatever I did the result seemed to be arguments and upset between me and Ron, and the situation was getting more intense. After yet another row over Garry, Ron said to me one morning, 'Right, I've had enough. You'll have to choose between him and me.'

I was flabbergasted. 'What do you mean? How can I choose between you?'

'Either you and the boys leave,' Ron said, 'or if you want to stay with me, then take Garry back to his dad. You know that's where he wants to be. I don't want to lose you, Maureen, but if you don't take Garry away, then we'll have to part. We can't go on like this.'

I knew he meant it. 'Just give me time,' I said. 'I need time to think about it.'

'All right, but you've got to make up your mind soon.'

My emotions were tearing me apart but I tried to think things through rationally. I couldn't bear the thought of losing Garry, my first child. I loved him. But then I loved Ron too. Despite the way he had changed, despite the fact that I was no longer happy with him, I was still in love with him and felt I could not live without him. It was certainly true that Garry was unhappy with Ron and wanted Tony. Was it fair to keep him from his own father? Graham, on the other hand, thought of Ron as his dad and would be upset and disturbed if he was taken from Ron. It was clear that whichever decision I took would cause me heartache, but at last I realised that I would have to take Garry back to Tony. It was the only way I could keep Ron and it might be better for the boy in the long run, although it would be torture for me.

I packed Garry's clothes and, leaving Graham with a friend, caught the bus into Basingstoke with Garry. We arrived at Tony's and he asked us in. I tried haltingly to explain what I had come for.

'Tony, Garry's been fretting for you. He isn't happy with Ron, he wants you. I want you to take him because we can't cope with him living with us any more.'

Tony was obviously completely taken aback, and I had to repeat my case several times. Then he said, 'I'll have him if you'll come back to me, Maureen.'

I had been expecting this. 'No,' I told him. 'There's no way I'll ever come back to you. I've got nothing for you, Tony. But Garry needs you. You're his father and you've got to take him.'

While we spoke Garry was looking from one to the other in bewilderment, and that really broke me up. At last I just got up and walked out, leaving Tony and Garry both standing at the door looking at me helplessly. I cried all the way to the bus stop. 'What kind of woman have I become?' I asked myself. 'How could I abandon my own child?' I knew that others would judge me harshly, and they did. My mother was very upset and could not understand my action. Some of the women on the site stopped talking to me when they found out what I had done and this condemnation, combined with my own guilt and sense of loss, made me deeply unhappy.

I soon found out that Tony was living with a woman who was taking good care of Garry. Although I longed to see my son I remembered how his father's visits had disturbed him and decided it would be easier for him to settle if I stayed away. I held on to the thought that when he was old enough to understand he would come and see me again. But for years I thought of him every day and it was particularly difficult whenever his birthday and Christmas came round, and I wondered what he was doing and if he was happy.

Garry's departure removed one cause of tension but now a new one appeared. A private detective turned up one evening and said that he was working for Ron's wife's solicitor. He wanted Ron to sign a statement admitting adultery with me. Ron was absolutely furious, for his wife had left him so many times for other men, while he had not taken up with me until after she had left him for good. Now she was suing him for desertion and adultery and expected him to pay her maintenance, not only for his own children but for the baby she had had since they had parted, which she claimed was Ron's. Ron looked ready to vent his fury either on me or the detective but we managed to calm him, and the detective persuaded him that it would be easiest if he agreed to admit adultery but challenged the paternity of his wife's youngest child.

It was months until the divorce hearing in Cardiff but Ron was in a black mood all that time, cursing and swearing whenever he thought of his wife. When he at last went off to Wales I was terrified that he might be provoked to violence when he saw his wife – might even murder her. Then again, he had once been very much in love with her and she sounded the sort of woman who could always get what she wanted from men. And she had his four children with her. Perhaps he would go back to her and I would never see him again. I didn't have a moment's peace until Ron returned. He was depressed and exhausted and didn't want to talk about his experience, but he told me that he had won his point over the maintenance of the baby and the divorce would be final in three months time. I tried to comfort him, but his wife had told him that he would never see his children again and he could not be consoled.

The divorce proceedings left Ron bitter and angry. He rarely showed me any tenderness and spent more and more time with his mates from the motorway, drinking and getting into fights. I knew that most of these men, married or not, went in for casual promiscuity, and I was afraid that Ron was being infected with their outlook. Our sex life now became a new focus of tension. Ron was becoming dissatisfied with me because, to me, sex was primarily an expression of my love for him and I wasn't interested in going in for anything out of the way. But Ron wanted more excitement; he even suggested involving other couples, or other women, in our love-making. I was torn between distaste and fear of Ron's rejection, but when I tried to please him by lying about how I felt, Ron saw through it and was angry with me.

I became pregnant again and I hoped that this would be a chance for Ron and I to repair the damage to our relationship. But it was not possible to undo the past. I no longer trusted Ron, especially where women were concerned. I was not the only one who found him attractive and I became jealous of his relationships with other women on the site. A girl called Lucy had moved into the next caravan with her little boy. She was easy-going, had a good figure, dressed provocatively, and it soon became apparent that she and Ron were mutually attracted. She used to come over to our caravan and I would have to sit there, pretending not to be aware of the eye contact between them. It was worse when Ron went over to her caravan for a chat. I was eaten up with jealousy, wondering what they were up to.

One day I went into Lucy's caravan for a cup of tea and recognised Ron's writing on a note that was lying on the bench. When Lucy wasn't looking I had a quick glance and saw the words 'I love you'. I was sick with misery and jealousy. I said nothing to Lucy but when Ron came home I taxed him with it. Ron said he had not meant it, he was just sorry for her as she was going through a bad time, and I should forget about it. I tried to believe him but he still went on seeing Lucy and one day, when I knew Ron was with her, I collapsed. A friend, Julie, took me into her caravan and called the doctor who told me that I was in danger of having another miscarriage unless I calmed down.

Julie and her husband, Roger, talked to me for some time, trying to persuade me to leave Ron. 'He's causing you so much stress,' Julie said, 'if you don't go now you're going to have a complete nervous breakdown and you'll lose the baby too.' I went home and spent days trying to decide what to do. I didn't want to leave Ron but I was so upset by the way he was behaving, and I was determined not to lose this baby. So one night I asked Roger if he could drive me and Graham to my Mum's. I had promised Ron in the past that I would never leave him but the situation had become impossible. I had already lost one baby and sacrificed my first child for Ron's sake, and I wanted this baby to live. As soon as my Mum had taken us in I told her everything that had been happening.

'You did the right thing coming here,' she said. 'You are both going to stay with me.'

My mother was very kind and understanding but I could not settle happily there. I missed Ron so much and, though I knew rationally that I had made the right decision, I was still miserable. My Mum grew impatient with me and would tell me to snap out of it. 'Even if you don't care about yourself think of the baby you're carrying,' she would say.

I went to see Ron's mother, who also lived in Basingstoke. Although I knew that she had not been a good mother to Ron when he was a child, and I was always being told what a hard woman she was, she had accepted me from the start and had never shown me anything but kindness. I was not sure how she would regard me now I had left Ron, but she told me, 'Look, Maureen, you're not to stop coming round to see me. After all, that's my grandchild you're carrying.' She told me that she had seen Ron who had said he was thinking of living with Lucy, but his mother had told him that if he did she wouldn't have her in the house.

One afternoon I had been shopping in Basingstoke and decided to pop in to see Ron's mum on my way home. I thought that there was something odd in the way she said 'hello', and realised why when I went in and saw Ron sitting on the couch. My heart missed a beat. As soon as I saw him all my love for him welled up again, and I forgot all the pain he had caused me. I just longed to be his arms. We greeted each other awkwardly and Ron asked me how Graham and I were.

'We're all right,' I said. Then I couldn't help adding, 'but I miss you.'

Ron asked me to go into the kitchen so we could talk alone. He told me that everything between him and Lucy was finished, that he had never loved her, and she was only looking for a good time. 'Will you come back?' he asked. 'We can make a fresh start.' I didn't bother with any pretence of hesitation. I had just been waiting for him to ask me and before he had even finished speaking I was in his arms. His parents were pleased about our reconciliation and when I went back to my Mum to tell her I was returning to Ron she accepted my decision, although she told me that I would always be welcome with her.

I now think that the Lord was with me both in my decision to leave Ron and my decision to return. He knew how much I could take, and that at that stage I couldn't cope with the situation. I needed that break away from Ron, but it also helped me to see that I couldn't live without him.

We settled down on the site again and were happy for a while but it wasn't long before the old routines began to re-establish themselves. I was now heavily pregnant and Ron was going out with the gang from the motorway again, and flirting with the young single mums who lived on the site. I began to get seriously worried when Ron started seeing a lot of one particular woman called Judy. I actually found a note from him in her caravan and it was as though the Lucy business was happening all over again, but this time, being almost due to have my baby, I could not leave.

Michael was born in Alton Hospital on 20th November, 1970. We were both thrilled with him. Ron would come into the ward with a bunch of roses for me, kiss me and then gaze proudly at Michael in his cot. With tears in his eyes he would whisper, 'Isn't he beautiful!' But I knew that Judy was looking after Graham when Ron was at work and that Ron was going to her for his meals. I was pretty sure that he was taking advantage of my absence to have an affair with Judy, and I often lay in my hospital bed crying, but said nothing for fear of losing Ron.

When I came out of hospital Ron behaved in a loving and solicitous way. He became determined that we should move. We had put up with the cramped conditions of the caravan long enough and it was time we found somewhere decent to live. One day Ron said he was going out and wouldn't come back until he had found us somewhere to live. He returned several hours later, triumphant.

'I've found us a bungalow to rent, Maureen. It's in Eversley. Two bedrooms, a garden, a garage, all furnished. We move in two weeks.'

Ever optimistic, I was sure that now our life would sort itself out. In Eversley the wounds of the past would heal and our love would blossom again. I may not have known the Lord in those days, but he was still able to bless me with one of the most precious things he can give us – the gift of hope.

6: Anguished years

At first it seemed wonderful to be in our own bungalow, with so much more space. Ron was excited because the large garage and garden meant that he would be able to keep birds. He started to breed budgies, and then added doves, pheasants and finches, until eventually the bungalow was surrounded by aviaries with around forty different kinds of bird. This was a side of Ron I had not known about and, while I couldn't personally work up a great deal of interest in the birds, I was happy to see Ron occupied with something so harmless.

I really believed that we would be starting a new life together, and that Ron would be different now that we were off the site and in a proper house. But it was stupid of me to think that a change of house could bring about a change of heart. Ron was the same man in Eversley as he had been in Hook. He was still working on the motorway and mixing with very hard men, and his values were their values. His temper was foul and I was used to being the butt of it.

The bungalow, which had seemed so perfect, turned out to be damp, and this affected Michael's health. Not long after we moved in, he came down with bronchitis and was taken into hospital. It was so distressing seeing him in an oxygen tent, fighting for breath, and I felt shattered after my visits to the hospital. Who could I turn to for sympathy and support but Ron?

'It's pitiful to see him, Ron. He looks so helpless.'

'Well, whose fault is it that he got bronchitis? You couldn't have wrapped him up properly.'

'I did, Ron. It's the house. You know it's damp.'

'The house! It's you – you're a hopeless bloody mother!'

Michael came out of hospital and I settled to a dreary routine. Again I was lonely and friendless. Ron worked long hours and I had nothing to do while he was away but take Michael out for walks in his pram, or sit in the bungalow and mope. Eversley seemed a desolate place. I could sit for hours looking out of the window and see nobody pass.

Graham started at the local primary school but after he had been there for a few months they told me that he was a very slow learner, and that it had been decided that Greencroft School in Farnborough would be a more suitable school for him. Greencroft was a special school, and my first reaction was to feel ashamed that my son was so different from other children that he needed a special school. Then I was worried about how I was going to get Graham to Farnborough every day. That turned out not to be a problem, for there was a school bus provided and all I had to do was to take him to the bottom of the lane where we lived, and make sure the bus picked him up. After I had seen the school, and when I realised how much more content Graham was there, I gradually stopped feeling ashamed and was just glad that he was happy.

I could have put up with my loneliness during the daytime if my relationship with Ron had been better, if I could have looked forward to his coming home each evening without fear of his moods and temper. One problem was that he continued to brood about his children in Wales. He used to go out to the garage and spend hours looking at his birds in silence, and I guessed that he was thinking about his children. When we celebrated our first Christmas at Eversley, Ron was generous as usual, but the atmosphere was spoiled by his sudden gloomy silences, as he wondered what kind of Christmas his other children might be having. I seemed unable to comfort him at these times; his pain went too deep. I even wrote to his ex-wife, begging her to allow Ron to see his children, but she did not reply.

Shortly after our move my divorce came through, and I found I was pregnant again. My fourth son, David, was born at the beginning of 1972. Ron and I were still not married and I was unhappy about this. We were both divorced, and the only reason I could think of why Ron would not marry me was that he didn't want me to have that hold over him. However, after David arrived, Ron too began to think that it was time to get married, for the boys' sake. Despite all our difficulties, I was still thrilled when we set off for Aldershot Register Office in March 1973, and I became Mrs Sims at last.

The difficulties between us went deeper than Ron's bad temper. Our sexual relationship was no longer a source of joy to me, but had become a source of fear and humiliation, and it was this aspect of our life that was at the heart of the years of misery and degradation that were to follow.

I had already realised, at Hook, that Ron wanted me to be a different kind of woman. In reality I was just a very ordinary woman who wanted a stable family life and a normal loving relationship with an affectionate and faithful husband. But in Ron's fantasies I was some kind of fantastic sex kitten, adept in every kind of seductive technique. He would come in at night hoping to find a scantily clad temptress waiting for him and, when instead he found a tired housewife, he would erupt with frustration and rage.

Soon after we moved I realised that Ron was still seeing Judy from the caravan site. He stopped making any pretence about it, and she began coming over to the bungalow, supposedly to visit both of us, but obviously just to see Ron. When I saw the loving way he treated her I was sick with jealousy. Ron admitted that he had been sleeping with her when I was in hospital having Michael, and that they made love when he took her back to her caravan after she had visited us. 'She's the kind of woman I like,' he told me, and I was terrified that he would leave me for her. When Ron suggested that the three of us should go to bed I was disgusted and wanted no part in it. But eventually my fear of losing Ron made me give in.

This affair ended but my own nightmare continued. I loved Ron so much that there was nothing I would not do for him, and I was always in fear of his leaving me. Although living with him had become a hell I could not contemplate life without him.

Ron always attracted women, and perhaps I could have learned to live with it if it had just been a matter of his having affairs. Although I was very jealous and was tormented whenever I thought Ron was with another woman, I could have put up with his infidelity and remained faithful to him. But Ron did not want this. He would have been furious if I had had a secret affair, but he wanted me to have involvements with other men, as long as these were arranged and organised by him. The young chap who picked Ron up in the works van every morning became a friend of ours. He often came round in the evenings, usually bringing some pot for us to smoke. When I was high on this stuff I was able to lose my inhibitions and behave in the way Ron wanted me to, dancing in a seductive way, and talking freely about sex. Ron loved this, partly because he enjoyed my being so uninhibited in front of his friend, who he knew was attracted to me. But when he began to suspect, quite without justification, that I was seeing this friend behind his back, he was incensed and indignant.

One evening the phone rang and I answered it to hear a strange man's voice addressing me by name. He said he had my number from someone who said I would be able to give him sexual gratification by talking to him over the phone. I was horrified, put my hand over the receiver, and told Ron what this man had said to me. Ron smiled. 'Go on then, talk to him,' he said, and I realised sickly that it must have been Ron himself who had put the man on to me. I managed to say the sort of thing that was required, conscious that Ron was listening and would be angry if I failed him. This was the first of many such calls.

We started going to parties nearly every weekend or having them in our own house. They were wild parties, more like orgies, with people smoking pot, drinking, and swapping sexual partners. At that time just about everyone we knew was involved with this sort of activity. I just didn't know any ordinary people living ordinary lives. I heard talk about 'the permissive society' and thought to myself that this meant that the life I was leading was normal. This was the way the world was now, I told myself, and my secret longings for a quiet family life were ridiculously old-fashioned.

Ron was becoming harder and increasingly bitter. His mother had died and his father immediately took up with a much younger woman, which made Ron furious. He began to be violent, which led to his dismissal from his job on the motorway. He moved to security work, then back to the motorway again. Over the next years Ron was alternating between security and construction work, both hard and stressful jobs. He became obsessed with his need for money, sex and power, and perhaps it was not surprising that he became involved in the pornography trade.

It was not difficult for Ron to find the right contacts. We used to go down to London and come back with cases full of magazines and films. Most of this Ron sold to his workmates on the motorway. We made a lot of money out of it, but after a while Ron heard that the police might be on to him so he stopped dealing so openly, though people still came to our house to watch the films.

After a violent episode at work, when he had threatened the company's agent, Ron was offered the choice of redundancy or transferring for a spell to the Shetlands, to work on the North Sea Oil contract. He chose to go out to Lerwick. I was lonely without him. He phoned regularly and he sounded like a different man, gentle and loving, telling me that he missed me and longed to be back. Although perhaps I should have welcomed this period as a brief respite from the problems of our marriage, I just didn't know what to do with myself when Ron was away. I sometimes saw my mother, but it was a long journey and our lives now had so little in common that it was harder than ever to talk to her. I spent most of the time dreaming of an ideal life with Ron – just him and me and the boys living together happily. I feel now that it was part of the Lord's plan to put me through this lonely time, partly as a much-needed rest from Ron, but partly to show me yet again that I couldn't live without him.

Ron was in a strange mood when he came back from Lerwick.

'I think I'm going off my rocker, Maureen.'

'What do you mean?'

'I don't know. It's just that I keep having these silly dreams . . . silly thoughts . . . as if God was talking to me . . . telling me I should become a preacher. Perhaps it's the devil getting at me, what do you think? It was so quiet and lonely out there, and I missed you, perhaps that's all it was.'

I seized on this explanation gratefully. 'Yes, it was just that place, being on your own so much. Enough to make anyone go round the bend! I'd just forget about it if I were you.'

This wasn't the first time Ron had talked about God. I never encouraged him, because it just seemed creepy to me. I knew so little about Christianity and I thought that an evil person like Ron couldn't possibly have anything to do with God. Nobody had ever told me that God loves even people like Ron and me, or that Jesus had come so that sinners could be saved.

Ron remained moody and jumpy for some weeks, and he was worried about money, for he was out of work now. Then he told me he had a new idea for making money.

'I could put a few women on the game. I know one or two who'd do it and I could get some more. You know they can earn forty or fifty quid an hour! I'd organise clients for them and take a good chunk of their earnings. Sound like a good idea?'

I was afraid to let Ron see how appalled I was. I knew that if he had these women around he would soon be involved with them himself. I could only see one way out.

'You don't want to get a load of strange women in, Ron,' I said. 'I'll do it myself. That way we'll keep all the money.'

I shall always remember waiting for my first client. A man phoned me on Saturday evening. He sounded polite and well-spoken, and he turned out to be a successful businessman. I trembled as I made the arrangements, trying to sound professional and nonchalant. I quoted the price Ron had told me to ask and we agreed that he would call on Monday afternoon.

I put down the receiver and told Ron about it.

'That's great, Maureen! I'll take the boys out on Monday afternoon, so you'll have the house to yourself, OK?'

'OK,' I said. I tried to smile but Ron detected the break in my voice and looked concerned.

'Look, are you sure you want to go through with this, Maureen?'

'Yes, Ron, it's all right.'

'That's my girl! Tell you what, let's all go out for the day tomorrow, take the kids, and have a good time. Take your mind off it.'

Although I was filled with trepidation I had not dared to back out, even when Ron seemed to be offering me the chance to do so. I knew he would resent it if I had, and would find some other woman to do the job. I was happy to see him so pleased with me. And also, I have to

76

admit, despite my revulsion and nervousness I had some sort of feeling of power, some pride in the fact that men were willing to pay so much for me.

On Sunday we went to Portsmouth for the day. Ron was in a really good mood, treating the boys to rides at the fair, and acting in a more loving way towards me than he had for a long time. I tried to enjoy myself but I was unable to take my mind off what was to happen the next day. What would he be like? What would he expect from me? Would I be up to it? I remembered those prostitutes I had met so many years ago when I worked at the Cumberland, and recalled some of the things they had told us about their clients. I looked at my boys and wondered if they would ever know what their mother had become. I thought of my own mother, and how horrified she would be if she found out.

Monday afternoon came and Ron took the boys out. My client arrived and I did all that was expected of me. The man was perfectly courteous; he paid me the agreed sum and did nothing untoward, apart from making me dress in some leather gear he had brought along. When the hour was up he said, 'That was wonderful. I'll certainly come again.' For a moment I felt that slight thrill of power and pride, but the next moment I felt defiled and unclean and the moment he had left I rushed to the bathroom to have a bath.

I just wanted to forget the whole thing but that night Ron made me tell him every detail of what had happened. This was to be the same whenever I had a client, for Ron was always sexually aroused from hearing what I had been doing. Not all my clients were as polite or normal in their tastes as the first one. I felt utterly degraded and humiliated but there was nothing that I refused to do. I was becoming a nervous wreck, but I could see no way out of the situation. I had lost all will of my own and was just a zombie, Ron's creature, who would do whatever he made me do.

After five or six months Ron saw how the work was affecting me and suggested that it was time I packed it in. He was now working full-time in security again, so our money problems had eased. I was now no longer formally a prostitute but Ron had got used to my sleeping with other men and he did not want to lose the stimulation he derived from this. When men friends of his came round to watch pornographic films they knew that Ron was quite happy for them to take me off to the bedroom. I never dared to refuse for I knew that Ron wanted me to do it.

Although at the time those months seemed to be the worst time of my life, on reflection I can see God's hand even in that situation. He allowed me to live like that knowing that one day the experience would help me to relate to women living similar lives, and to help them as nobody who had not been through it themselves would be able to do. And I also realise that, nightmarish as that time was, it might have been worse. Most prostitutes are regularly beaten up by clients, and few escape contracting diseases, but the Lord spared me from those particular horrors, and when he saw that I could take no more, he rescued me from the situation.

The problem of the damp in the bungalow remained with us. Michael was now suffering from frequent asthma attacks, and David had begun to be affected too. The bungalow was in a bad state of repair generally, the landlord refused to help and we became desperate to move. We were on the council housing waiting list, and Ron also called in the sanitary inspector. We were not optimistic, but we had a lucky break, for the council were looking for a security worker for a site in Hartley Wintney. Ron was approached, and told that a three-bedroomed house would be available.

I was really excited. Hartley Wintney is a pleasant village, bigger than Eversley and less isolated. I would be that much nearer to my mum in Basingstoke. As soon as we could, we all went off to look at the house. It was a newly built house and I loved it as soon as I saw it. After years of cooking in cramped conditions I was particularly impressed by the large kitchen/diner.

'It's lovely, Ron. Do let's take it.'

'All right, love. I'll get in touch with the council right away.'

'What about furniture though?' I asked, for the bungalow had been furnished, and this house was unfurnished. 'We'll need carpets too.'

'Don't worry, we'll get everything we need. I'll have to sell off some of the birds anyway, and the money will help.'

I was touched by Ron's willingness to give up his birds, and by the enthusiasm with which he set about ordering carpets and furniture for our new home. He really did care about the family, and was anxious about the boys' health. The one soft spot in Ron's hard and ruthless nature was his love for children. He found it difficult to show love, never having received it as a child, but he was, in his way, protective towards the boys. When I hear now about young children being sexually abused by members of their own families, I realise that there were limits to Ron's depravity. He was always very anxious that the boys should know nothing of what was going on in the house; the parties were held and the pornographic films were shown late at night when they were safely in bed. Having had such a tough and loveless childhood himself, Ron did not want our sons to suffer in the same way. His aggression and violence in the home was directed at me, rather than the children.

Another new start, I thought, and again I dreamed that now things would be different. This time, at last, it would be just Ron and me, and the boys, a normal happy family. Of course, it was not like that, and I was stupid to think that anything was going to change. I was still tormented by Ron's incessant sexual demands and his aggressive behaviour when I failed to come up to his expectations. He still wanted to involve other people in our sex life, and not long after we moved he told me he had met a couple who were willing to swap partners on a regular basis.

I was very jealous when Ron told me about Karen, for she was apparently unhappy in her marriage, and I was afraid I would lose Ron to her. I had no desire to sleep with her husband but, as always, I agreed to whatever Ron suggested. I was told that Ron would go to Karen's house, while Peter, the husband, would come to me. I was relieved when I met Peter and found he seemed to be a really nice person. But however nice he was, I still didn't want anyone but Ron, and eventually, because I could see that Peter was a sympathetic man and wouldn't be angry, I admitted this to him.

'You know, Peter, I'm only doing this because Ron wants me to. If it were up to me I wouldn't. Nothing against you – I like you – but I love Ron and I don't want anyone else.'

Peter looked at me with tears in his eyes. 'To be honest, Maureen, it's the same with me and Karen.' So we just sat and talked until it was time for him to go.

Ron was full of enthusiasm about Karen and I was relieved when she and Peter moved, and the situation ended. But the wild parties started again and, if anything, things became even worse than they had been in Eversley. I was so harassed by all this pressure, and by the worry that I was abnormal – hopelessly old-fashioned or even frigid, as Ron often suggested – that I began to go to pieces. I felt rather as I had when I was a young wife with my first baby. I just couldn't cope with life; I couldn't cope with the children; I wanted to lock myself away and not have to face anyone. I actually took an overdose at one time, but a neighbour called the doctor and I hadn't taken enough to do me any serious harm. I praise God now for saving me, but at the time I did not care whether I lived or died. The doctor told me I needed tranquillisers. I took the Valium he prescribed, but they failed to calm me. No pill could solve my problems, or ease the mental anguish I was suffering. On Valium I found that I was just as unhappy and unable to cope, but I was also sleepy and forgetful.

I gave up the tranquillisers, but now I turned to drink in an attempt to numb my pain. I became friendly with Pat, a young woman who lived near us. She was divorced and had four children, and drank heavily. I began to drink with her, and I found that the combination of Pat's companionship and the alcohol gave me some comfort. Drink also made me less inhibited and more able to please Ron. The trouble was that Pat was always involved with men. She used to ask men from the building site in for drinks. Of course, I got to know these men too, and I realised that we were both regarded as easy.

One of the men who came to Pat's regularly started to pay me particular attention, and I became quite fond of him. One day he came round to my house when Ron was at work. I wouldn't let him in, but Ron arrived home just as he was leaving.

'Who was that bloke who just left?' he shouted.

'Oh, that wasn't anybody, Ron,' I said, trembling, for Ron's face was white with rage.

'What do you mean, it wasn't anyone? Stop mucking me about! Don't you dare lie to me.'

'He's just someone I see at Pat's. He wanted to see me but I wouldn't let him in.'

Ron stormed out, slammed the door. After a while he returned, still in a furious temper. 'That bloke's had it,' he shouted. 'Terry and Bob are coming with me tomorrow and we're going to sort him out.'

I begged him not to make trouble, but this served only to incense him more. The next day, Ron's mates Terry and Bob turned up and they went off to the building site, Ron muttering, 'I'll kill him, I'll kill him'. I was petrified, but luckily the intended victim saw Ron and the others coming and escaped. Afterwards I heard that he blamed me for 'leading him on' and I was afraid to go to Pat's or even to go out of the house in case I saw him or any of his mates, who were apparently out to get me.

How had I got myself into such a mess? All I ever wanted was love, someone to care for who would care for me. Just as, when a lonely child, I had wished for a real friend, now I wished for a faithful, loving man. 'If only I could meet someone who would love me and me only,' I used to say to myself. Although I loved Ron, I had stopped thinking that he could ever be the caring man I dreamed of, who would love me alone, for his aggression and infidelity seemed to be an ineradicable part of his character. And yet, though Ron had many opportunities to leave me for another woman, he never did so. And though at least one of his friends tried to lure me away from Ron, I resisted the temptation to escape my situation in that way.

I did sometimes contemplate leaving Ron, though, and once, when I was completely at the end of my tether, I phoned the Samaritans, who put me in touch with a women's refuge in Basingstoke. I spoke to a woman there who arranged to pick me and the boys up the next morning. Though I was apprehensive about the refuge I was determined to go, but that evening Ron came home in a sweet and loving mood, seeming like a different man. I couldn't think of leaving him when he was behaving so tenderly towards me, and in the morning I phoned to say that I would not be coming. By the end of that day Ron was back to his old self, but I felt that I had had my chance and lost it, and could not leave now. I often wondered why it was just on that one evening that Ron had changed his normal behaviour and so prevented me from leaving him. Now I am sure that it was the Lord's work. God kept us together throughout those miserable years, knowing that our desperate and destructive relationship would one day be transformed into real love.

7: *Heartache*

Once my youngest child started school I started to look around for a part-time job. I felt that if I were completely alone in the house all day my nerves would give way completely. I was lucky to find work in an antique shop in the village, and I stayed in this job for more than ten years. My employer was a Jewish man, a Mr Lazarus, and he was always extraordinarily kind and considerate to me. I am quite sure that my coming to work for him was the Lord's doing, for I needed some way to get away from my problems at home. I also needed a friend, someone right outside of my situation who would be sympathetic and understanding, and Mr Lazarus proved to be such a friend. Although he was often under pressure in the shop he always sensed when I was upset and needed help. He would stop everything, make me sit down with a drink, and have a quiet talk.

One night I left my house at midnight, having had a row with Ron, and started to wander aimlessly around the village. Mr Lazarus was just saying goodnight to a friend, and saw me. He took me in and talked to me gently until I had calmed down, and persuaded me to go back home. I thank God now for arranging that meeting, for if I had not met Mr Lazarus that night I don't know what I might have done. Although he knew something of what sort of life I led, and he must have known of our reputation in the village, this man never treated me with anything but respect. My relationship with him was like an oasis of normality in the chaotic world in which I was living.

Ron was still overworking, living at a hectic pace and barely sleeping, and it was obvious that his health was suffering. On top of everything else he had become involved with a football team that he was coaching and playing with. He agreed to play in a charity match on August Bank Holiday 1977. The night before we had been to a party and Ron had returned looking pale and exhausted. He must have been in desperate need of sleep but we spent half the night in furious row, about sex again. It ended as usual with me shaking and crying and Ron threatening and abusive.

As we approached the football field the next day Ron was pale and shaking. I couldn't see how he was possibly going to play in that state; he looked as though he were near collapse. I wanted to tell him he should back out of it but he seemed determined to play and I knew that nothing I said ever had any influence on him once he had made up his mind.

Ron seemed to be all right at first but I soon realised that he was playing badly. The others started shouting 'Come on Ron, you're letting us down!' He missed a penalty; all his movements were getting slower and it looked as though he was finding it an effort to run. At last the game ended and Ron staggered off the field. His hand was clutching at his chest and the next moment he was lying on the ground. His mates picked him up and I followed fearfully as they carried him to the clubhouse.

I sat holding Ron's hand as we waited for the ambulance. He was conscious but in great pain. The ambulance drivers gave Ron oxygen, and I continued to hold his hand, weeping, as we drove to Frimley Park Hospital. I kept thinking that it was all my fault. If I had been more accommodating I could have warded off his anger the previous night – then he would have had more sleep and perhaps this would never have happened.

He was rushed to the intensive care ward immediately, and I was shown into the waiting room. After a while I was summoned to the sister's office where I was told that Ron had had a heart attack. My tears started afresh. There were two insistent thoughts in my head: that Ron was going to die and that it was all my fault. I was taken to see Ron in a cubicle where he was lying wired up to an ECG machine, and with a drip in his arm. They had given him a morphine injection and he was no longer conscious.

'There's nothing you can do, Mrs Sims,' the nurse told me. 'You'd better go home now. Leave your phone number so that we can contact you.'

'But is he going to be all right?' I whispered.

'Well, it's really too early to say,' she admitted. 'But he's going steadily now. Try not to worry.'

I returned to the football ground to let Ron's friends know what had happened. They were all so kind and concerned. Then I picked up the boys from the friend that was looking after them, took them home and gave them tea.

'Where's Daddy?' they kept asking.

'Daddy's not very well. He's in the hospital.'

'When's he coming home, Mum?'

I wished I knew the answer. I tried to reassure them and not let them see how frightened I was, but the moment they were in bed I broke down. I cried myself to sleep and as soon as the morning came I phoned the hospital. I was told that Ron's condition was stable but that there was no point in my visiting him yet.

After two days Ron was out of intensive care and I was able to visit him every day until, after ten days, he was discharged. He was told that he must take things very easy and try to change his lifestyle, cutting down on smoking and late nights. I prepared a bed downstairs for him. It was distressing to see him so helpless, frightened to move in case the pain attacked again. But gradually his strength returned, and as it did so he became increasingly frustrated by his enforced inactivity, and he began smoking heavily again. After a matter of days he had another heart attack and was taken to Basingstoke Hospital.

He seemed to be in even greater pain than with the previous attack. He went through the same routines of drip, heart monitor machine and injections. I was terrified that this time he would not pull through, but again he survived. I knew the doctors had warned him severely that he must avoid stress if he did not want to bring on angina or a third heart attack. I wanted to add my voice to theirs but I was afraid to say too much in case I made Ron angry, and afraid even of showing how worried I was, in case I caused him extra stress. I had the idea that a third heart attack was always fatal and I was so anxious to avoid anything that might provoke one.

Ron returned home again to a bed downstairs. He had been told to avoid worry, but the doctors had also insisted that he must not return to work for a long time, and so he was made redundant. It was impossible for us not to worry about money. My part-time job did not pay enough to support a family. We were so touched when some of Ron's mates from work came round to see him and one of them shyly produced a wad of notes.

'We had a bit of a whip round,' one of them said, 'I think it's £250.'

Ron broke down after they left. I was afraid of his getting too emotional, because of the strain on his heart. I hugged him and said, 'There you are, we'll manage, darling. Everything's going to be all right.' I wanted to calm him but I, too, was very moved. These men had all suffered from Ron's violent temper, and they knew just what sort of life he led. What was it about Ron that inspired such loyalty and affection despite his countless faults?

When Ron became stronger it was suggested to him that he attend Egham Rehabilitation Centre, as a first step to getting back to employment. I was glad of the break during the days, although I worried whenever Ron was out of my sight in case he might have another attack. After six weeks at Egham he was told that they considered him ready now to undertake any work that would not be too taxing physically. He had been put through all kinds of tests and had done extraordinarily well, and this boosted his confidence. Within two weeks he had found a job as a security supervisor at Fleet.

It was good to have Ron working again and money coming in, but this job was certainly not ideal as far as his health was concerned. The hours were long and he had a lot of responsibility. Also it brought him into contact with some of the men we had been involved with before, and the round of parties started again.

I had thought that the only positive aspect of Ron's illness was that it would force a change of lifestyle. After the second attack he gave up smoking and I hoped we would lead a quieter life. But he continued to read and sell pornography, and we were soon back to the lifestyle that went along with that. Although Ron had been forbidden sexual intercourse, as putting too much of a strain on his heart, he was still totally obsessed with sex.

In a way things were even worse than before, for now Ron was frustrated and depressed and felt threatened in his masculinity. I was sorry for him but unable to help; as Ron's obsession with sex grew, so did my fear of it. I had thought that if Ron could not have me he would not want anyone else to, but it turned out that this was not the case. One night when Ron was out, Chris, one of his friends came round. Almost immediately he started to make sexual advances to me. I repulsed him, and he said, seeming genuinely surprised, 'What's up? Ron won't mind.'

'Please go away,' I said. 'I don't want this. I only want Ron.'

Chris smiled and said, 'Yes, but what does Ron want?'

I felt sick. I managed to get rid of Chris but I knew that if this was really what Ron wanted I would have to give in eventually. And of course I did. Whenever one of Ron's friends came round I started to tremble and feel sick because I knew what they were expecting of me, and I knew that I was powerless to resist. My love for Ron and my fear of him had turned me into his puppet, and my own weak personality had become almost totally submerged under his strong one.

The long hours he was working, the worry over his health, and his frustration was making Ron's temper more inflammable than ever. Our relationship deteriorated further and I stopped expecting anything from Ron but threats and abuse. One night I was woken by him holding a knife to my throat. 'Take this away from me,' he said, 'because if you don't I'm going to kill you.' Sometimes I thought that it was inevitable that one day Ron would kill me. Sometimes I thought about suicide.

One Saturday afternoon Ron and I and the boys were sitting in the front room, having returned from a football match, when there was a knock at the door. I went to open it and saw a young man there who was a stranger to me.

'Hello,' he said. 'I'm Steven.'

This meant nothing to me. 'Steven who?' I asked.

'Steven Sims,' he answered, 'Ron's son.'

I left him standing in the hallway while I went to prepare Ron for this surprise, for I was immediately concerned about the effect of a shock on Ron's heart. I quietly explained to Ron that his son Steven had come to see him. Ron leapt up and rushed out to the hall and in a moment he and Steven were locked in an embrace. Ron was quite overwhelmed. He had never forgotten his previous family but had resigned himself to accepting that he had lost them for ever.

He welcomed Steven in, and as soon as he was sitting down with a cup of tea he asked him to tell us about his life and about the other children.

Steven told us that his stepfather had treated them badly and that the older children had all been thrown out of the house as soon as they left school. He had been living rough for three years. His sister Tina had married at sixteen, disastrously, but was now remarried and had a little girl. Ron was quite taken aback to hear that he was a grandfather! I could see how distressed he was when he heard that the middle boy, John, had been in trouble and was in Borstal and that Mike, the youngest boy, had been in care.

Ron called me out of the room for a moment.

'Maureen,' he whispered, 'I want to offer Steven a home with us. Do you think we could manage?'

'Of course we could,' I replied. 'We could squeeze all the boys into the bigger bedroom and put Steven into the little room. Go and tell him now.'

I was so happy for Ron that he had found his son again and I was prepared to treat him as though he were my own child. Steven moved in with us and the following weekend he and Ron went off to Cardiff where Ron was able to meet Tina and Mike. I met all Ron's other family before long, and I loved them all, for they were a part of Ron.

When he was in Wales, something Tina had said made Ron suspect that Steven had been involved in criminal activities and, working in security, it was not difficult for him to make enquiries. It turned out that Steven had been involved with his brother John in a burglary and had jumped bail. We could get into trouble for harbouring him, and Ron managed to persuade him to give himself up, promising that he would accompany him to court and speak for him. Steven was lucky for he was given bail in our custody, and at his trial the judge decided to give him a chance and not send him to prison. He was fined and returned to live with us.

Ron was happy to have his son with him and I wanted to do all I could for Steven. I was sorry for the boy. He had had so little love in his life, and I wanted to make it up to him. I waited on him and really gave him more care and attention than I did my own boys. But Steven's past had too great a hold on him, and the love and care he was now receiving was not going to change his character. He had no interest in getting a job and he took up with a rough, hard-drinking crowd. Many a time I waited up for him when he had been out drinking, undressed him and put him to bed. He took advantage of us in many ways and he made it clear that he was jealous of Ron's love for our three boys. He also tried to come between me and Ron, and his presence was the cause of still more friction in our already fraught relationship.

In the end we reluctantly decided that Steven would have to go, Ron had always been protective of the children but Steven was not bothered about what effect his behaviour might have on them. Graham was now eleven and we were afraid of Steven's influence on him. Steven was not particularly upset or surprised when Ron told him he must go, and he went off quite happily to live with some friends he had made in Fleet.

The long hours and comparatively poor pay of Ron's job were getting him down and he went back to construction work, as a foreman on the Odiham Bypass. He was earning good money and he was feeling much happier. He now felt perfectly healthy so stopped taking the drugs he had been prescribed. As the money started coming in, Ron was able to build up his aviary again and he began to think about our moving to Devon in a few years and starting a bird farm there.

Then, one Friday night in May 1980, Ron was just finishing a meal after his return from work when he suddenly screamed and collapsed onto the floor.

'Maureen, it's happening again,' he gasped. 'The pain . . . I can't stand it! Get the kids out of the way,' for the boys were frightened and crying, 'Daddy, Daddy!'

I rushed to the phone and called the doctor. I was distraught, for Michael was having a bad asthma attack at the same time. The doctor arrived in no time and immediately gave Ron a morphine injection. He sent for an ambulance but told me to stay at home. There was nothing I could do and he could see I had my hands full with Michael. I felt so helpless. When I tried to hold Ron's hand and kiss his forehead he pushed me away, because he couldn't breathe.

I stood weeping as I watched the ambulance drive Ron off to Basingstoke Hospital. 'Don't let him die, please don't let him die,' I was saying, but I had little real hope. I was convinced that a third heart attack was inevitably fatal and I was sure that this was the end. I tried to calm the boys down and we sat and watched television until they went to bed. When I phoned the hospital I was told that Ron was in intensive care.

I lay in bed unable to sleep, just chanting to myself, 'Don't let him die. Don't let him die. I love him, don't let him die.' I can't really say that I was praying, for I knew nothing of God, and didn't know who I was addressing. All I knew was that I loved Ron, despite everything, and I didn't want to live without him. At last I fell asleep but was wakened almost immediately by the phone ringing. I looked at my watch and saw that it was five o'clock. Trembling, I picked up the phone.

'Mrs Sims?'

'Yes, is that the hospital? Is it my husband?'

'Yes. Can you come to the hospital as soon as possible please. Your husband's in a critical state.'

In a daze I woke up the boys, relieved to find that Michael was better. I rushed round the corner to a friend and asked if he could take us to Basingstoke. We drove first to my mother's house, for I wanted her to be with me, and then went on to my aunt's where we left the boys.

At the hospital we were told that Ron had not only suffered a heart attack but early that morning had had an infarct, which meant that his heart had actually stopped beating. He had temporarily 'died' but they had managed to resuscitate him. We went in to see him. There were drips in his arm and an oxygen mask over his face. Mum and I sat crying by his bedside, and suddenly he gained consciousness and recognised me.

'Hello, darling,' he managed to whisper. 'Have my budgies been fed?'

'Yes, of course. Don't worry about your birds, love, I'll take care of them,' I said. 'Just you relax and get better. We want you home again.'

My mother left to see to the boys and I phoned all Ron's family. Steven came immediately and went in to see his father. While he was in with him we heard bells ringing and saw doctors come hurrying from every direction towards Ron's room. Steven rushed out looking terrified. 'I don't know what's happening,' he said. 'Dad went all blue and they chucked me out.'

A nurse came and led me off. 'Sit down, Mrs Sims,' she said. 'I'm sorry to have to tell you that your husband has had another heart attack.'

'Is he alive?' I gasped.

'Yes, but he's in a very critical state. We're doing all we can but I'm afraid we can't guarantee anything. We'd like you to stay here overnight.'

I felt that I wanted to be on my own so the family left, but later that evening Ron's brother Barry arrived. He spent the night in the waiting room so that he would be available if I needed support. I wasn't able to be with Ron because they wanted him to have undisturbed rest. I was quite unable to sleep, for every moment I was expecting a knock at the door. I actually imagined a couple of times that I heard a knock and jumped up to find that nobody was there. In the morning I was totally exhausted but relieved that, as nobody had disturbed me, I could assume that Ron had survived the night.

I went to the waiting room to find Barry drinking a cup of tea. He had spent the night stretched out on two armchairs and he tried to cheer me up by telling me how he had woken up to find three nuns standing over him. 'I thought I'd died and gone to heaven,' he said, and I managed a laugh, glad to have him there for comfort and support.

As I walked towards the intensive care unit I was met by the sister. 'How is he?' I asked.

'His condition is no longer dangerous,' she told me, 'but he needs absolute quiet and rest. You can see him but we think it's best if he has no other visitors for the moment.'

I was so thankful. I could hardly believe that Ron was really out of danger, that he wasn't going to die. Two days later Ron was moved to the recovery ward. He was still in pain and very sick but I could see him improving a little day by day.

Two things happened over that period when Ron was in hospital. His father had a heart attack and died. We did not tell Ron about this until after he had left hospital, for we were afraid that the stress might be too much for him in his condition.

The other episode was that I was befriended by a nun who was visiting her brother in the hospital. She was very kind to me and told me that she was praying for Ron and that she had asked her church to pray for Ron as well as for her brother. When Ron was well enough to receive visitors she went in to see him and I could see afterwards that he was affected by his talk with her. He was quiet and thoughtful, and even asked me to pray for him. Ron left the hospital after ten days and, as he left, we heard that the nun's brother had died.

Ron was in many ways a changed man when he left hospital. He had been so near death, and he was very shaken by the experience. He had to take things very easy as any physical exertion brought on pains. Despite this he returned to work, against the doctors' advice.

There were no more parties now, but as Ron was back on a strict regime of rest, we returned to the situation of his seeking vicarious sexual satisfaction. Again his friends started coming round, wanting me, and again I gave in. I hated it and each time hoped that it would be the last, but I felt that I could not deny Ron anything. I was afraid of making him angry, not just for my own sake, but because I feared that any extra stress or frustration might bring on another attack. At the back of my mind was the constant fear of his death and I felt that I must allow him anything that might give him pleasure.

Before long Ron started to suffer with angina and he was sent to see a heart specialist who suggested that he go into Southampton General Hospital for tests. These would establish whether he needed to have a heart bypass operation. Ron underwent an exploratory operation and various tests at Southampton for six days. Some of the tests were quite gruelling, and Ron was alarmed when one of the other men in with him had another heart attack while waiting for his operation. When the six days were over, the consultant went from bed to bed delivering his verdict. I could feel Ron's tension as he approached us. But he was smiling. 'Good news, Mr Sims,' he said. 'I see no reason to bypass your heart. One of your arteries has been narrowed but the rest aren't too bad and the muscle round your heart isn't as badly damaged as we'd expected. I'm quite optimistic about your future.'

It seemed that another miracle had happened, and at that moment we seemed so close. But things soon returned to normal and Ron went back to the Odiham Bypass. When he was in construction work he mixed with the most rough and foulmouthed men and his own manners and language always sank to the same level. At that time I took on an extra job as a cleaner in the offices of the construction company Ron worked for. The men always used to laugh and joke with me and the other woman who worked there, and one night we went into one of the caravans to have a cup of tea with the men. It was all perfectly harmless, but apparently word got round to Ron that I was considered easy, and he was absolutely furious with me. I felt I was unable to do anything right. Ron usually liked other men to admire me and, if I had flirted a little with these men, it was only so they would think Ron was lucky to have a wife like me. I left the job soon after, as I felt uneasy in the situation.

A new cause of stress came with the news that Steven had been convicted of arson and had been sent to Borstal. This news, combined with the hard work and long hours, was too much for Ron. His angina attacks became more frequent and more severe and, when the doctor said that it was imperative that he give up work, he was forced to agree. It seems to me now that the Lord allowed Ron to have those heart attacks and the angina to force him to slow down his destructive lifestyle. I know, too, that Ron's life was saved so miraculously after his fourth attack because God had a place for him in his kingdom and work for him to do.

Ron's leaving the motorway work was a relief to both of us, and in many ways we were happier. But money was a worry, as we now had only Ron's pension, besides my earnings. Ron was often in pain and often very depressed. It was so sad to see a man who had formally been so strong, lively and energetic brought so low. Sometimes he would cry and say, 'I'm finished, my life's over. I'm no good for anything now.' The greatest heartbreak for him was having to sell his birds. He hated to see them go and the hobby would have been good for him now that he had so much time on his hands, but we needed the money.

Ron had become very dependent on me and physically I was getting very tired, and increasingly despondent about what the future held for us. Ron's illness had made me realise just how much I loved and needed him, but our marriage was still as insecure and stormy as ever. It was just the thought of how much the boys needed me that kept me going.

Ron needed something to occupy him so I was pleased when he got interested in the local Cubs and Scouts. He became involved in fund-raising activities and also started coaching the Cub's football team. He had always got on well with children and he started to become really enthusiastic about the Cubs. It was the highlight of his week when he went off to watch them playing football. As far as I was concerned, I was glad to see Ron happily occupied with what seemed to be a harmless activity. I could not have guessed that it was to lead to a sequence of events that would change our lives completely.

8: A new creation

One Saturday morning, when I came in from work, I was greeted by Ron looking happy and excited.

'Maureen, you'll never guess what happened to me this morning,' he said.

'No, love, I can't guess,' I yawned. A couple of Ron's friends had come over the night before and we hadn't got to bed until the early hours. I tried to work up some interest in what Ron was saying.

'When I was down the Cub hut this morning I met this bloke, Trefor Jones, the Reverend Trefor Jones,' Ron said.

'Who?' I asked. It sounded as if he had said 'the reverend' and I thought I must have misheard.

'The Rev Trefor Jones. He's the Baptist minister. There's a Baptist church in the village, and he's the minister. Anyway, I got talking to him this morning and he's coming to see me after lunch.'

I really thought Ron had gone mad. I had never met or talked to any sort of clergyman, but I imagined them as very strait-laced and holy people. I thought that the only people who could mix with them would be people who were very good and never did anything wrong. How could we have a minister in our house? The people who came to our house were prostitutes, drug addicts, alcoholics, and hard-drinking, foulmouthed, promiscuous construction workers. I remembered Ron's raving about being a preacher and God talking to him, and wondered if he was getting the same crazy ideas again. Well, as soon as this minister person discovered what an evil man Ron was, and found out what sort of life we led, he'd certainly want nothing to do with us!

As the afternoon went on I could see Ron getting jumpy and restless. He kept looking at his watch and walking round in circles. I felt sorry for him. He'd been so enthusiastic about this chap coming, and now it looked as though he was going to be let down. I put my arm round him and said, 'Look, love, why don't you phone him? He's probably got some good reason for being late.'

As I finished speaking, there was a knock at the door and Ron rushed to open it, I heard a voice saying, 'I'm so sorry I'm late,' and then Ron's voice saying, 'Come in'. I was in the kitchen at the time but after a moment or two I went into the front room and Ron introduced us. I was surprised by the man's appearance. He looked just like anyone else and was dressed in ordinary clothes. I had thought all ministers wore black clothes, or a dog collar at the very least. I shook hands and said, 'Hello' nervously. I didn't know what to call him. Should I call him 'Reverend' or 'Reverend Jones' or what? I made them some tea and retreated into the kitchen.

They went on talking for hours. The boys came running into the kitchen for their tea and I hissed at them, 'Shh! Don't make a noise! There's a minister in the front room talking to your dad.'

'What's a minister?'

'Why's he talking to Daddy?'

'What are they talking about?'

'I don't know,' I said impatiently, 'They're just having a chat.' I was as curious and as bewildered as they were.

At last I heard voices in the hall and came out. 'Trefor's just leaving,' Ron said. Trefor! Had Ron really called him by his first name?

The minister smiled at me. 'Goodbye, Maureen, I hope I'll be seeing you in church tomorrow.'

I smiled vaguely and said goodbye. See us in church? Me and Ron go to church? That was hardly likely!

Ron was quiet for the rest of the evening. Trefor had left him some pamphlets and he started leafing through them. But then he said he fancied an early night and, as I was very tired, I was happy to agree. I wanted to go straight to sleep but Ron kept talking, telling me about what Trefor had been saying. It really sounded like a load of rubbish to me. He was going on about Jesus and about sin and things like that. I didn't know what he was talking about but at least he seemed happy and he wasn't talking about sex as usual.

Then Ron produced a book and opened it. I looked at the cover, surprised to see him reading. It didn't look like a pornographic book. It was a paperback called *Hell's Angels,* by someone called Brian Greenaway.

'What's the book,' I asked sleepily.

'It's something Trefor gave me. It's really good. About this bloke that used to be a Hell's Angel.'

Ron continued to read as I drifted off into sleep. While I slept peacefully beside him, Ron was having an experience that was to change his whole life. He read how Brian Greenaway, a tough, violent person, much like Ron himself, had met with Jesus when he was in prison. The thing that struck Ron most was that Brian said that Jesus had forgiven all the evil things he had done. Ron had never known that Jesus had died so that even the most wicked person could be forgiven and reconciled to God. He had thought that he was too bad a person ever to be forgiven, that he had gone too deep into sin for it to be possible to start afresh. Now he realised that he could start a new life and put the past behind him. When he finished the book, Ron had tears streaming down his face as he prayed a simple prayer of repentance, and surrendered his life to Jesus.

Sundays were my usual time for catching up on the housework, so the next morning I was ready to start my chores. But as soon as Ron came down he said,

'Come on, Maureen, get the boys up. We're all going to church.'

Trefor had said something about seeing us in church, but I didn't for a moment expect that we would go. I called the boys and, though they were as bemused as I was, they were surprisingly willing to come with us. I felt nervous as we approached the church. I had no idea what to expect. Would I be able to cope with it? Would I know when to stand up and sit down? Would people talk to us? What would our friends say if they knew where we were going?

The church was an old and rather decrepit building. Trefor had done wonders in renovating it, as I came to understand later, but it was still in a pretty bad state of repair, and my first impression was that it was a real dump. There were only a few people there, but they were all very friendly and welcoming, and I gradually started to feel less uncomfortable. Trefor appeared and the service started. It was a simple enough service, and I was relieved that nothing was required of me, and it wasn't obvious that I had no idea of what was going on. There were hymns, prayers, and Trefor preached. I let it all wash over me, not really listening. I found it rather boring, but at the same time, I had a sense of inner peace.

As we left, Trefor shook hands with us and said, 'See you at six-thirty,' and Ron replied, 'Right, we'll be here.' Church twice in a day? I still couldn't understand what had happened to Ron, but then I remembered that two of his friends were expected that evening, and I hoped the service would go on long enough for us to miss them. Ron's friends coming round was still something that I dreaded, and I was happy to go to church if that meant I could get out of the situation.

Ron was talking about the church all day. He told me what Trefor had told him, about our village chapel being a daughter church of Camberley Baptist Church, and Trefor having been taken on to rebuild the fellowship in Hartley Wintney. He also tried to tell me what had happened to him.

'I'm a new person now, Maureen. Jesus has made me a new creation. I've been forgiven for all the bad things I've done, and I can start a new life now.'

This all sounded like rubbish to me, and I didn't really listen. But I couldn't help noticing that there was a difference in Ron. He hadn't used a single swearword all day, and he was gentler in his manner towards me and the boys. We went off to the evening service, and afterwards stayed and had a cup of tea and a chat; as in the morning, I was struck by how friendly people were, though the actual service still meant nothing to me.

I had a job getting the boys off to bed. They were really excited about having been to church. It was such a new experience for them. While I was upstairs with them, I heard a knock at the door and looked down to see Ron opening the door to his two friends. They were holding bottles of drink. My heart sank as I heard Ron asking them in, and then call to me, 'Maureen, Tim and Chris are here.'

I went downstairs reluctantly. They were all sitting in the front room. As I came in, Ron turned to his friends and said, 'I've got something to tell you.' The three of us looked at him expectantly. I had no more idea of what Ron was going to say than they did. 'There aren't going to be any more parties,' he said firmly, 'I've become a Christian.'

'You what?'

'What do you mean?' Tim and Chris both looked astounded.

'I've given my heart to the Lord Jesus Christ,' Ron said. 'I've finished with my old life and I'm going to start living in a completely new way.' And he went on to tell them more, about how his sins were forgiven, and he was a new creation, and so on. I stopped listening and just concentrated on the one thing that had really hit me. No more parties! Had Ron really said that? I could hardly believe it. Tim turned to me and asked, 'What do you think about all this, Maureen?' I didn't answer at first; I was still stunned. Then at last I said, 'I want whatever Ron wants.'

Tim and Chris looked at each other, then slowly rose. 'Well, Ron,' Chris said, 'I admire you in a way for this, but don't try to get me to join you. I'm perfectly happy with my life; I enjoy it. Come on, Tim, we'd better go.' And, still clutching their bottles, they left. I looked at Ron and then threw my arms around him.

'Ron, I'm so proud of you. You really mean it? No more parties?'

'Right. No more parties.'

'And Ron . . . does that mean I won't have to go with other men any more?'

He nodded. 'Or . . . or any other women?' I asked falteringly.

Ron held me to him. 'Yes, love, from now on it's just you and me.'

Tears of joy and relief poured down my cheeks. I could hardly believe what I was hearing. That night, as we lay in bed, holding each other tightly, Ron said, 'Maureen, I'm so sorry for the way I've treated you over the years. All I can say is that things will be different now. We're going to have a new life in Jesus.'

I was so happy. I would never have believed that Ron would ever apologise to me. And he had said that it would just be him and me now. I had longed for this for years, but never believed that it would happen. When I had wished for a man who could love me and me only I had not dared to hope that that man could ever be Ron himself. He was becoming the loving, tender man that I had dreamed of.

As Ron had promised, our life changed completely. Trefor was frequently in our house, reading the Bible with Ron, and bringing him books. Our life began to revolve around the church and its activities. Ron was like a different man, but I couldn't help having the nagging doubt at the back of my mind: is this going to last? I think the one event that really persuaded me that Ron's whole attitude to life had changed fundamentally was when he decided to dispose of the hundreds of pounds worth of pornography that we still possessed. He obviously wouldn't sell it, and he didn't want to give it away. Even throwing it away was unsatisfactory, for someone might find it and be harmed by it. So he and Trefor took the cases of books and magazines to the ground at the back of the church and burned the lot. Ron came home with smudges of soot on his face but looking completely at peace. When he told me what he had done I hugged him. 'I don't really understand what's going on,' I told him, 'but I know you've become the man I always wanted you to be.'

Christmas 1982 was quite different from our usual Christmases, which were normally just an excuse for overindulgence in food and drink. Ron became very involved in the carol service at the church, for the whole Cub pack and their parents had been invited. People in the village became friendlier. Everyone noticed the change in Ron. Even his face had changed; it had become softer and lost its hostile, defensive look. I was happier than I had been for many years. But I still found the church services boring and, however much Ron talked about it, I hadn't really understood what the gospel of Jesus was all about. Ron never put any pressure on me to make any personal commitment and it never occurred to me that I might. I just regarded Christianity as something that Ron had become involved in. I was deeply thankful for the way our lives had changed, but I still thought that the cause of this change was just Ron's affair, not mine.

Then, on New Year's Day, Trefor came round to tea, and to watch a video of *The Ten Commandments*. After it had finished, Trefor turned to me and said, 'Maureen,

tell me what you think about how Ron has changed.'
I thought for a bit and then said. 'Well, to be honest,
Trefor, I can still hardly believe it. He's changed so
much. All the hate and the bitterness has gone and he's
stopped swearing. It's just wonderful.'

'Maureen,' Trefor said. 'You can become a new person too. Would you like that? Would you like to give
your heart to the Lord and ask him into your life?'

I swallowed hard. The fact was that I wasn't really
interested. Admittedly, Ron had changed in a miraculous way, but then he had always had this lurking
interest in religion, whereas I had never been bothered
about it. Despite being involved in the church now, I
was not much more interested in Christianity than I had
ever been. But how could I refuse Trefor? I was never
any good at saying no to anyone, and I hated the thought
of hurting Trefor's feelings when he had been so kind to
us both.

'Yes, Trefor,' I said. 'I would like Jesus to come into
my life.'

As Trefor prayed with me, I saw that Ron's eyes were
filled with tears and I realised how much he, too, had
wanted this.

Trefor and Ron were both thrilled, and told me what
joy there was in Heaven because I was forgiven and
would have eternal life. The old Maureen Sims had
gone. I was now a born-again Christian and a new
creation in Jesus Christ. I was happy that they were
so happy, and I did feel a sense of peace. But I cannot
pretend that I immediately felt different or understood
the commitment that I had entered into. However, in
the weeks following my conversion, I started to read the
Bible properly for the first time. I read the gospels and,
through them, I came to know and love the Saviour that
I had accepted.

Up until then I had never tried to pray, other than
reciting the Lord's Prayer. But now I began to ask
the Lord for my own personal needs and those of my

family and my new brothers and sisters in him. I asked particularly for boldness and the ability to communicate, and my faith grew as I realised that the Lord could actually change me into a stronger person. I was so grateful to God for what he had done in our lives, because the way things had been going I might have ended by killing myself, and Ron's heart might have carried him off. We had been rescued from death and hell through God's saving grace. But the work of the Holy Spirit was greater than redemption alone. I had seen how Ron had changed and I now saw myself gradually becoming a different woman, one who could actually talk freely to people, for the Lord gave me the right words to say. The feeble, frightened woman, who could hardly open her mouth, had become someone who, with the Holy Spirit's power, could actually give help to others.

Ron was already deeply involved with the life of the church and now I, too, began to find work for myself. I started visiting sick and needy people and found no difficulty in chatting to them and cheering them up. I started helping at the women's meeting, just making tea to start with, but gradually taking on more responsibility. It was a very small fellowship and many of the members were elderly, so new people willing to be energetic in the work of the church were more than welcome.

The change in us had been noticed not just in the church, but in the village as a whole, I had always walked with my head down, frightened to be recognised, in case people knew of our reputation and the things we were involved in. Now Jesus was telling me that I was no longer that sad, guilt-laden woman, but that I was his child and he would guide me and protect me. No wonder I was now able to walk with my head held up, and feel free to greet my neighbours with a friendly smile!

Everyone in the village must have known about Ron's conversion, for, almost immediately, he had become involved in door-to-door evangelism work with Trefor. They must have noticed the change in our marriage, too, for now we were always together, as a couple or as a family. When once we had walked the streets shiftily, carrying cases of pornographic books, now we walked them boldly together, carrying Bibles.

It was my relationship with Ron that was the greatest blessing to me. Now the bitterness had gone from his life, he was able to love and trust me as he had never allowed himself to do before. There was a new light in his eyes when he looked at me, and he constantly told me how much he loved me. We became like a courting couple, walking about hand in hand, lost in our love for each other. In a way it was as though our marriage had only just begun. Miraculously, all the horrors of the years we had spent together just dissolved, and we began a new commitment to each other. And as our love grew daily, so did my faith in the Lord who had brought about these wonders.

One day when Trefor and Ron had returned from visiting in the village, our youngest son, David, ran up to his father and said, 'I want to give my life to Jesus, Dad, like you and Mum. And Michael wants to as well.' Trefor prayed with them, and Ron and I were so full of joy that they had made this decision. It was wonderful for us to see them learning to read their Bibles and praying, growing in the Lord daily. They had to put up with a lot of teasing at school but they curbed the instinct to retaliate. Ron and I were confident that Graham, who was now fifteen and the only member of the family who had not accepted the Lord, would soon follow in his brothers' footsteps.

Ron had already given his testimony and spoken in various churches, but I was very surprised when both of us were invited by Chris Russell, the minister of Camberley Baptist Church, to give our testimonies there on Mothering Sunday. I was extremely nervous about speaking in front of so many people, but I knew that it was what God wanted me to do, and I prayed that he would give me the courage I needed. Even Ron was nervous on the day, and I was quaking. We were led into the vestry, where Chris Russell and the deacons prayed with us. Before we went out to face the congregation, a sister called Molly called me aside and said, 'Jesus loves you and his Holy Spirit is going to talk through you. I will be sitting at the front and praying for you.'

As I looked out over the large congregation I felt my nerves attacking, but I fought it. I knew that God was with me and I could see Molly sitting in the front and smiling at me. I had written my testimony down so that I wouldn't actually dry up, and once I had started I found that my nervousness subsided and I was speaking quite naturally. I told them something of the sort of life that I had known, and how Jesus had saved me from such wretchedness and despair, and given me a new life and a new husband. When I finished I sat down with tears in my eyes, whispering, 'Thank you, Jesus. I couldn't have done that without you.' Then Ron got up and spoke, at much greater length. At the end of the service everyone shook hands with us, and many people said kind things. I felt so happy doing something like this with Ron, as a couple. Our marriage had changed so wonderfully that I still sometimes felt as though I was in a dream.

Before long, Trefor came to us and said, 'I think it's time that you both got baptised.' Ron and I both responded enthusiastically, and immediately decided that we would like to be baptised together. In the weeks following, Trefor came to see us regularly to explain just what baptism meant, showing us the relevant Scriptures. When he told us that baptism was a matter of obedience to Jesus, who had told us we must be baptised, and had been baptised himself, I felt that I could hardly wait to give this public sign that I was ready to follow Jesus for the rest of my life. We asked Trefor to explain why we had to be totally immersed, and he told us that this was a symbol of burial of the old life and rebirth to the new. Although we both already felt that our old sinful selves were behind us, we liked the idea that the waters of baptism would cut us off completely from the old Ron and Maureen Sims.

I was really excited as the day of our baptism approached. I invited my mother to the service, and also my boss from the antique shop and his secretary. I didn't expect Mr Lazarus to accept, as I thought a Jew might feel uneasy about going to a Christian church, and I was thrilled when he promised to come.

We were to be baptised on the evening of Palm Sunday. After the morning service, my mother arrived and we had lunch. Mum joined us in saying grace before the meal and I saw tears in her eyes as she heard our boys praying. For years she had watched helplessly as my life had become more and more wretched, and she must have feared that her grandsons would turn out like their father. Now she saw us as a united, happy, loving family and, while she might not have understood how this miracle had happened, she rejoiced in it.

We all walked down to the chapel at six o'clock. Ron and I went to the back to change, him into white shirt and trousers, me into a white dress. As we came out I saw that the building was packed and I spotted my boss, smiling at me from the back of the church. I gave a short testimony, feeling very emotional, and I ended with the words, 'I love the Lord Jesus with all my heart,' as tears streamed down my face. Ron gave his testimony and went on to preach a gospel message. As I walked down the steps of the baptistery, I felt as though the Lord was bearing me up. Trefor baptised me and, when I walked back up the steps, I had a wonderful sensation of cleanness and new life. All the filth and shame of my old life had gone for good and I was a new creation in Christ.

That Palm Sunday was one of the happiest days of my life. Many were moved by our testimonies and Ron's preaching and two women gave their lives to Jesus that evening. Perhaps what touched me most was when Mr Lazarus ran up to me and gave me a kiss on the cheek, saying, 'May God bless you both, and may he make you very happy.'

9: Cancer

The Lord was teaching me to live from day to day relying on him. Perhaps it was easier for me than for more successful people to realise how helpless we are without God. I knew what a mess I had made of my life before I let him take it over. I was finding out for myself the truth that nothing is impossible for God, as I found him blessing me with abilities that could only have come as a gift from him. He gave me the intellectual capacity to read and understand his word in the Scriptures, the fluency and sensitivity to talk to and help others, and the strength to tackle any work he might ask me to do.

From making tea at the women's meetings, I went on to doing the reading, and eventually leading the meetings. I became involved in door-to-door work, but probably the work I was most involved in was the children's club at the church. When I started helping there it was a small group, but it built up to about forty children. It was tiring work but I felt it was very worthwhile. Some of the children were real terrors and difficult to control, but I knew that their home backgrounds were often deprived or violent. My heart went out to them, knowing what my own sons had been saved from, by the grace of God. The children came to trust me and would come to me with their problems, and I was usually able to help them.

To our great joy, Michael and David, at the age of twelve and eleven, had asked to be baptised, and many were blessed by the simple testimonies they gave at their baptism. A few months later, some Americans came over to lead a mission and, after they led a special service in our church, Graham was one of those who responded to the appeal to make a commitment to the Lord. We were so thrilled that our whole household now belonged to Jesus! But before long I became so involved in church work that I actually began to neglect my own family. Ron was always busy now, taking his testimony and the gospel message into churches, schools and youth clubs. When he was at home I was often out, and we started to see less of each other. I believed that God's work had to be church work or helping other people, and I did not connect it with my own role as a wife and mother. But then the Lord told me clearly: 'I have given you a husband and children, and my work for you includes looking after them.' I realised then that I had been confused about my priorities and, from then on, I made sure that I met the needs of my family first, and then turned to God's work for me outside the home.

In the autumn of 1984 I received a letter from my doctor asking me to come and see him as soon as possible. I phoned the surgery and was given an appointment for that evening. I could not think why the doctor wanted to see me so urgently, but I didn't feel at all worried.

I was called into the doctor's room and, after asking me to sit down, he said, 'I'm afraid I have bad news for you, Mrs Sims. You remember you had a cervical smear test recently?' I nodded, and he went on, 'The results have come through and it has been verified that you have cervical cancer. We don't know yet how far it has gone, or what stage it is at, but we would like you to go to Basingstoke Hospital to see a specialist.'

I walked out of that surgery feeling much as I would have if the doctor had told me that I had a slight cold. Somehow Jesus had taken away all fear, and the word 'cancer' held no horrors for me. When I told the boys they were devastated, but I calmed them down, saying,

'Don't worry. We'll just take each day as it comes,' and that evening we went down to the children's club as usual. My boys must have told the other children what had happened because all evening they kept coming up to me and saying, 'Don't leave us, Mrs Sims. We love you.' I was very touched but I tried to reassure them that Jesus would look after me.

When Ron came home and heard the news he was surprised at my calmness. 'Quite honestly, I feel a fraud,' I told him. 'I'm sure there's nothing wrong with me.' In fact, I never said to myself at any stage, 'I have cancer' because I felt that if I admitted it, then the devil would start getting to work, creating fear in my heart. I felt sure that whatever was wrong with me, God would be able to heal, and I just didn't feel any anxiety. I continued to work, and carried on with all my normal activities; I had no pain.

The next week Ron took me to Basingstoke Hospital, where I saw the specialist. He didn't really tell me anything that my own doctor hadn't already told me, but said that he would like me to come in for tests the next week. I went in for the tests and was then summoned again to see the specialist. He told me that the cancer was malignant, it was in the third stage, and was spreading through my body. They would take me into hospital for a cone biopsy operation, but there was not much that they could do.

The news could hardly have been worse, but I still felt perfectly calm and cheerful. The worse my condition was, the more glory to Jesus when he healed me! I had not heard much preaching about healing at that stage in my Christian life, but I never doubted the Lord's power to heal. I had only to read my Bible to see him bringing miraculous healing to sick and needy people time and time again. Why shouldn't he do the same for me?

It was the beginning of November when I went into Basingstoke Hospital for my operation. I was taken to a ward where I had to sit on a bed and wait for the doctors to see me, and for a nurse to come and take a blood sample. There were other women in the ward, also sitting on their beds, and as I waited I looked at their faces and realised that all of them looked unhappy and frightened. The Lord said to me, 'I am with you and I will be with you all the days of your life, so keep your eyes on me.' And I thanked Jesus for being my Lord and Saviour, knowing that without him I would be just as frightened as these other women. After the doctors had seen us, we were allowed to mingle and chat. The women wanted to know why I seemed so cheerful. Wasn't I going to be having an operation the next day? I felt the Lord saying, 'Tell them about me,' so I said, 'Yes, I am going to have an operation, but I'm not frightened, because a very good friend of mine is going with me – a friend called Jesus. He loves me and he's going to look after me.'

Ron came that night to visit me. We sat holding hands and he said, 'You're going to be all right, love.'

'Yes,' I said. 'I know. Jesus is going to heal me.' Ron prayed for me and, before he left he kissed me and said, 'I love you, darling'. As I waved goodbye I thought how our love had grown and blossomed, and it seemed to me that if Jesus could have brought about this miraculous change in our relationship, he could certainly deal with my illness. I was given a sleeping pill, so that I would be sure to have a good night's sleep. I read my Bible and thought of all the people who I knew were praying for me. The night before, we had gone to a service at an Anglican church where they were moving in the Spirit, and people had been so kind, and had prayed for me. I felt perfect peace as I fell asleep.

The next morning I awoke to the brisk voice of a nurse saying, 'No breakfast for you, Mrs Sims, you're the second to go down to theatre.' I might have been going to a cinema, rather than an operating theatre, for I felt as though I were on cloud nine. As they put on the white gown and gave me an injection, I was overwhelmed with elation and joy. I heard a nurse's voice saying, 'Just lie quietly, now. They'll be along with the trolley soon to take you down.' But far louder was the voice of the Holy Spirit saying, 'I will be with you'. Two orderlies arrived and put me on the trolley and, as we went down the corridor. I was laughing and joking with them. One of them looked puzzled. 'Mrs Sims, you're going down for an operation, and you don't seem in the least nervous. Why are you so happy?'

'You see, I have Jesus with me,' I said, 'I'm a Christian.'

Outside the doors of the theatre I was put onto another trolley and, as the anaesthetist gave me my injection, he said, 'I can't believe how relaxed you look, Mrs Sims. You'll be going in there in just a moment'.

'Yes, but Jesus will be with me all the time,' I murmured as I lost consciousness.

When I woke I was back in the ward. Something felt wrong and I soon realised that I was unable to move. I was used to having backache, for I had had spinal problems for eighteen years, ever since having my first child, and had suffered from backache on and off since then. But this was obviously more serious. Apparently, while my legs had been up during the operation, a spinal nerve had become trapped, and I was now partially paralysed. During the day, I spoke to doctors who told me that it might be five or six months before they would be able to do anything about my condition, and it was possible that I might not walk again. But I still felt calm and free from fear, confident that my Lord would heal me.

When Ron came in that evening and saw the state that I was in, he was obviously shocked. But I told him not to worry and, when he saw that I was still able to laugh and joke, and that my faith was firm, he began to relax. As we were talking, we heard the woman in the bed opposite say to her husband, 'You see that woman over there? Well, she's got cancer and she's paralysed, and just look how happy she is. She says it's because she has Jesus in her life. When I get out of here we're going to church!' The woman in the next bed asked Ron and me to pray for her. She was desperately worried about her son, who was on drugs, and I had told her of the work Ron was doing with youngsters who were in trouble.

When Ron came in the next evening he told me that there was a woman waiting outside who would like to pray for me. Her husband was an Anglican minister who Ron knew slightly, and he had phoned to say that his wife had had a vision telling her that she was to lay hands on me and pray in the name of Jesus and that I would be healed. 'I'd like you to let her pray,' Ron said. 'You know I believe in the healing power of Jesus, and that he died for our sickness as well as our sins. "By his stripes we are healed."' Ron fetched the woman, and they put the screens round my bed and laid hands on me, praying in Jesus' name that I would get up and walk, and that all signs of cancer would vanish.

When they left I lay on my back, still unable to move, but feeling great peace. I took up my Bible and began to read from Luke Chapter 13, verses 11 to 13: 'There was a woman who had had a spirit of infirmity for eighteen years; she was bent over and could not fully straighten herself. And when Jesus saw her, he called her and said to her, "Woman, you are freed from your infirmity". And he laid his hands upon her, and immediately she was made straight, and she praised God.'

I thought to myself, eighteen years, that's just now long I've had trouble with my spine. While I was reading, I became aware that I needed very badly to go to the loo. I rang the buzzer for the nurse to bring a bedpan, but nobody came, I rang again, thinking how odd this was, for the buzzer was always answered almost immediately on our ward. Still no answer. Then I heard a voice saying, 'You are healed – get up and walk.' I lay still for a moment and then I felt that I would be able to move my legs if I tried. Slowly, I lifted my feet, and moved my legs off the bed, and to the floor, where I felt for my slippers. As I rose and began to move, I could hear excited shouts from the other beds, 'Maureen's walking! Look at Maureen – she's walking!'

I walked down the corridor to the loo, and then went to the phone and called Ron. 'Ron, I'm up on my feet! I can walk!' I said, and told him what had happened. 'Praise the Lord!' Ron said fervently, and then added, 'Look, you'd better hurry back to bed. There'll be a right commotion if they see you've gone.' Sure enough, as I put the phone down, one of the nurses bore down on me, crying, 'My goodness, whatever are you doing, Mrs Sims? Get back to bed this moment before you have a fall!'

I knew that there was no need for me to be in bed, but I did as I was told. When I got back to bed all the women were in a state of excitement. 'Did it happen because of them praying for you tonight?' they asked, and I said yes.

The next evening Ron came in and was thrilled to see me walking about. He told me he had been phoning all our friends to tell them what had happened last night, and they were all praying for us, because tonight we were expecting to hear the result of the operation. At last the doctors came to talk to us. They told us that, although all the tests had indicated that I had cancer, the operation had shown that there was nothing wrong apart from a blood disorder and some abnormality of the cells. 'There's nothing there that a complete hysterectomy won't cure completely,' they told us. We hugged each other, and the tears flowed. I was going to live! I didn't have cancer!

We left the hospital praising God for his goodness to us. I was satisfied that our prayers had been answered but Ron's response to the situation was, 'God hasn't finished yet'.

For some time we had been wondering whether we were in the church that God wanted us to be in. Trefor had married and moved away from the village, and we missed him very much. His absence had meant that Ron had greater responsibilities in the church, but he was experiencing a sense of spiritual emptiness, and we both felt that we wanted more from our church life.

The fellowship at Hartley Wintney had become very dear to us, and they were kind and loving people, but so many of them seemed to be 'once-a-week Christians'. And, in a way, Ron was too much for that little Baptist fellowship; many found his bold and outspoken manner too extreme and disturbing. Grateful as we were for all that Hartley Wintney Baptist Church had meant to us, we were looking for more life, more depth, in worship and in teaching. Also, we were worried that the boys were becoming bored and restless in the church, for there was little in the services to attract young people.

Various circumstances led us to the King's Centre in Aldershot, a church built in a converted cinema. The first time we went to a service we were overwhelmed. The power of the Holy Spirit hit you as soon as you entered the building. It was a huge church with hundreds of people, and all of them seemed to be just overflowing with the love and joy of the Lord. The worship was wonderful: people were clapping and dancing, there were guitars and tambourines. We knew immediately that this was the church that we wanted to be part of, the church that God had led us to.

It was difficult to tell the people at Hartley Wintney that we were leaving the church. I was tempted to feel that they wouldn't be able to do without us, but I had given up all my work there before going into hospital, and we both knew that this move was what God wanted so we shouldn't have any anxieties over it. As we started to get involved in the life of our new church, and got to know the fellowship and the leadership team, we had no doubt that we were in God's will.

When I had left the hospital, Ron had said that God's work on my healing was not yet finished. He was right. Just before Christmas we had to go back to the hospital to arrange for me to go in for a hysterectomy. When we saw the doctor he said that he was absolutely amazed by the results of my tests; there was nothing wrong with me. I did not need a hysterectomy. When he examined me he said he could not even see the scar from the biopsy operation, and that internally I looked like a sixteen-year-old girl!

I had never admitted to having cancer and I had never doubted that God would heal me. Now I knew that he had honoured me for my faithfulness. I could not wait to go out and tell others what the Lord had done for me. If God could do this for me, he would do it for anyone who put their full trust in him and his healing power.

10: Stepping out in boldness

There was never any doubt in our minds as to whether we had done the right thing in moving to the King's Centre. It was quite clear that this was God's will for us, for we were greatly blessed by the worship and the fellowship there. The teaching was so powerful we couldn't get enough of it, for we felt we were growing in the Lord daily.

My only difficulty with the church at first was that they all seemed so wonderful that I felt inadequate. I used to look around at all these radiant Christians and think they were all holy, perfect people with no problems, and I could never hope to be like them. I confessed my feelings to a friend, and she laughed at me.

'Don't be silly, Maureen,' she said. 'We're all human here – none of us is any more perfect or holy than you are! And we've all got our problems and worries, too, just like you.'

I soon realised that this was true. People were so friendly and open at the King's Centre that we soon made many new friends and, as I got to know people better, I found that they all had their faults and their problems. But there remained another area where I felt inadequate. I seemed to be one of the few people in the church who did not speak in tongues.

I had not heard very much preaching about the Holy Spirit and I had assumed, when I heard of the baptism in the Spirit, that this must have happened to me when I went through the waters of baptism. But from the teaching I was now hearing, I learned that this baptism was a gift: the gift Jesus had promised to give to us when he returned to heaven, a gift that would bring us great power. One night at church, people were invited to go up for prayer for baptism in the Holy Spirit. Ron went forward, and I went with him. When they laid hands on Ron, I held on to him, and, as I did so, I found myself speaking in tongues. I felt power and joy welling up inside me, and from that moment I found a new strength to do God's work.

During the next few months two different evangelists, Reinhard Bonnke and Ray McCauley, prophesied that we were to be used mightily by God in spreading the good news of Jesus, and setting the prisoners free. These prophesies chiefly concerned Ron, but I was included in them. I certainly felt prepared to be used, and was happy to accompany Ron whenever possible. But the two younger boys were still at school and I felt that my priority was still to be there for them every day when they came home. Also, I still had my part-time job. We needed the money from this, and I still enjoyed it. My manager was struck by how changed I was, how happy and relaxed, and I lost no opportunity to tell him about my new life.

I felt content at that time to concentrate on my family, for I was still basking in the new, loving relationship that Ron and I had developed, and we were being taught by the Holy Spirit how to bring our boys up in a Christian home. I realised that any kind of pressure on them would be counter-productive, so I never nagged them about reading their Bibles or praying. That way I knew that when they did these things of their own accord it was because God was prompting them to, and that he would teach them whatever they needed to learn. I became much closer to the boys than I had ever been. Though I had always loved them, there were times when I just felt I couldn't cope with them, or couldn't be bothered, and I would send them away from me. Now

I always had time to talk to them, and I thanked God that they felt so free to open up to me, to discuss their problems, and even confess their faults. I handed all their problems, and all the other difficulties in our family life, over to God and let him sort them out. I knew he wanted the best for us all, and would never fail us.

Ron's ministry was growing now and he often had to be away from home. I no longer worried or moped in his absences as I had once, when I had been unable to trust him. I knew that he was doing the Lord's work, and although I missed him I was happy to let him go. I would sit by the telephone reading my Bible, waiting for Ron to phone and let me know how the meeting had gone.

Ron had given his testimony at the King's Centre, and twenty-six people had been saved as a result. About two months after that, I felt the Lord prompting me to consider giving my own testimony there. God told me to ask Mike Pusey, the senior pastor, if he would pray about this, and I did so. Soon Mike called me and said that he believed I should give my testimony at a Sunday evening meeting in May. I was very nervous about facing so many people, but before the meeting Ron and Mike prayed for the glory of God to shine through me. After I had been speaking for a few minutes, the Holy Spirit took over and conquered my nervousness, and I spoke freely of all that the Lord had done to change my life so miraculously. Afterwards, Mike preached a short sermon and appealed for people to come forward and receive the salvation of Jesus Christ. Sixteen people responded that night.

After a few months I started to become restless. I accepted that my family needed me, but I began to feel that God had other work for me in addition to my role as wife and mother. After all, I had been through so many bad times in the past, surely I could now use those experiences in reaching out to others. I knew how much needless suffering there was in the world, and my heart reached out to these people, particularly the prostitutes, drug addicts, alcoholics, and others who were living through the same kind of hell that Ron and I had been rescued from. I wanted to tell them that there is help at hand, there is someone who loves them and can give them peace and a new life. I felt ready to go wherever the Lord would send me with this message, but I was impatient for the call to come. I began to wonder if perhaps I was mistaken about God's will for me, and he did not have such a ministry for me at all.

I approached Margaret Pusey, Mike's wife, and told her something of what I was feeling. She arranged to come and see me one afternoon to talk and pray about it. We spent some time chatting about the family and how I felt I would like to be used by God. Then we held hands and prayed that if I was to be used then doors would open for me. After Margaret left I felt more content, prepared to wait patiently for the Lord to act in his own good time.

The next day there was a letter by a late second post. It was posted from London and I saw it was from Von, a sister in Christ. I read it quickly and then rushed to the phone.

'Margaret, I've just had a letter. I've been asked to do two meetings – one in London and one in Kettering.'

'Praise the Lord!' was Margaret's response.

'I never thought, when we prayed yesterday, that I'd have an answer so quickly.'

'Never underestimate God, Maureen. If he wants to use you, he is able to make it happen.'

Ron, too, was thrilled when he came in and I told him the news. He said immediately that he would drive me to London. I was so built up in my faith by this answer to prayer that I had no time for nervousness about addressing the meetings. I was quite prepared to stand in front of hundreds of people to share what God had done for me. Sometimes I looked back to the timid, weak-willed wreck of a woman that I had been and thought that she would not recognise herself in the woman that I had become, through God's grace. It was miracle enough that I had been saved from sin and degradation, but I could never marvel enough at God's blessing me with a strength and boldness that was so far removed from my old personality.

Once the first door had opened, it seemed as though doors were opening everywhere. Alan Richardson, one of the leaders at the King's Centre, who had now moved to Dorset, invited us down there, and asked Ron to help him with some outreach meetings he was arranging. Some of these were in small villages but Ron also spoke in the huge Poole Arts Centre. I particularly remember that meeting because I walked into the hall while Ron was testifying and, just seeing and hearing him, I broke down in tears. They were tears of joy and gratitude to God for changing the evil man who had brought me so much misery into a kind and loving husband, and one that I could feel so proud of. I could only thank God and give him the glory for the powerful speaker Ron had become, who was being used as a channel of the Lord to bring people to repentance and salvation.

I had seen my role on this trip as just being a support to Ron, but I was asked to do a women's meeting with Pat Richardson, Alan's wife. The only part Alan and Ron were to play on this day was to make tea and coffee and serve the women. They were happy to do this humble task, mindful of the Lord's words in Mark chapter 10 verses 43 to 44: 'Whoever would be great among you must be your servant, and whoever would be first among you must be slave of all.'

As at so many of these meetings, the hall was filled with those who were already saved, but there was just one woman there who was not a Christian, and after I had given my testimony she committed her life to the Lord. I learned later that her marriage was on the rocks and she had been suicidal, but after accepting Jesus she was prepared to start a new life with his help. After this woman had responded, I sensed that the Lord was asking me to call the women out for prayer. My first thought was that I couldn't do it; it was something I had never done before. But a moment later I was able to say to God: 'Lord, if that is what you're saying, then all right, I'll do it.' I called for all those who were in need of prayer to come forward, and I was surprised how many came, needing healing or deliverance. As I laid hands on them and prayed in the name of Jesus, I felt the power of the Holy Spirit surging through me. Some women fell to the floor, overcome by the Spirit's power; many were healed or delivered to the glory of God. It was a wonderful day, and one that taught me a lot. I learned that if we are willing to step forward in boldness, we need only take the first step and the Lord will do the rest.

My ministry developed in three main directions. As the boys grew older, I was increasingly able to accompany Ron and help with his ministry; then there were the meetings that I led in my own right, and a quieter but very fulfilling ministry of one-to-one counselling with women.

With Ron, I travelled all over the country and went into places that I had never dreamed of visiting. One of these was Charterhouse, the famous public school, where Ron addressed the boys. After the meeting, over coffee, a man came up to talk to me about healing, and he asked Ron and me to pay for him to receive the Holy Spirit. This man was the school chaplain, and that was just one of many times that the Lord used us to help people who, by the world's standards, were so much more privileged than ourselves. But 'God is no respecter of persons', and the social divisions that seem so powerful to us mean nothing to him.

A very different experience came in November 1986, when Ron was asked to speak at Wellingborough Youth

Custody Centre. We were met by the prison chaplain, a real man of God whose whole life was devoted to helping the boys. As he led us through the bleak corridors, and each door and gate was locked behind us, I was inwardly praying for Ron. This was all so strange to me, but only too familiar to him, and I was concerned about how it might affect him to be reminded of all those bitter years that he had spent in prisons. We were taken to the chapel, where I was introduced to the governor. I was to sit with him while Ron was preaching.

There must have been at least a hundred boys sitting in the chapel, with many warders strategically placed among them. I felt very depressed by the atmosphere and it broke my heart to see so many of the boys looking so frail and lost, not at all the popular image of young criminals. I was fighting back the tears, but when Ron stood up to speak everything changed. The boys heard him in total silence and seemed to be fascinated by what he had to tell them of his past life and how he had found the forgiveness and love of Jesus. As Ron talked of the love of Jesus, I looked at those pale, drawn faces and thought how many of those boys hardly knew what love is. I was sure that, with many of them, the main reason they were now locked up here was that they had been deprived of the love we all need if we are to grow up with any self-respect and compassion for others. Jesus touched many hearts that morning through Ron's ministry and, when we shook hands with the boys before they went back to their cells, we saw that many had tears in their eyes.

As we left, I turned round and saw some boys waving to us from their cells, and I felt so sad that while we had our freedom, they had months or years to face in that place. My heart ached for them. I thought of my own sons, and I wished I could go back and give a motherly hug to some of those lads who had known so little love in their lives. That evening we met the chaplain again at church in Wellingborough and he told us that some of the boys had asked to see him so that they could receive Jesus into their lives. I returned home with a real burden on my heart for all men and women and youngsters in prison. I prayed that we would have further opportunities to go into prisons and tell hurting people that Jesus can heal their broken lives.

That was the first of many visits to prisons and youth custody centres. One that I particularly remember was Rochester. Ron spoke there one Sunday morning and twenty-six boys came to the Lord. But for me the best thing about this visit was that we were able to stay and talk informally to some of the boys afterwards. I heard so many heartbreaking stories from those lads. I remember asking one boy about his family.

'I've got no family,' he said.

'Then what will you do when you get out of here?' I asked. 'What are your plans?'

'I dunno . . . I suppose I'll have to do something that'll get me sent back here. This is the only place I know.'

We can only pray that there will be more and more of God's people reaching out to such young people and telling them the good news of Jesus, not just when they are in prison, but before they start to get into trouble. It is because of that thought that Ron and I are both drawn to schools work. Ron and I have been into many schools and it's sad to see how few of the kids there have even heard of Jesus. We are mainly asked to go into schools to warn the youngsters of the dangers of drug abuse, but I have also spoken to the girls of the moral and physical dangers of early promiscuity. We have had letters from some of the kids thanking us for our talks, and saying how they were helped by the straightforward way we dealt with these issues.

I am always glad to be able to talk to the youngsters one-to-one, though I have heard things that made me weep, and I can only ask Jesus for strength and for the right words to say to them. One young girl came up to me and told me that she had been abused by her father, but that her mother hadn't believed her. She was now living with an aunt, and, though she had come to know Jesus, she was suffering badly from a sense of not being loved or wanted by her parents. I told her to talk to her parents, to try to understand the guilt they were probably experiencing, and to tell them she loved them. We prayed together and she said she felt much happier, just having talked to someone about it. I received a letter from her a few weeks later saying that she had followed my advice and was now able to talk to her parents freely. They had become more loving towards her and she was very happy as she was about to become engaged.

We spent one exhausting but fulfilling week at a tent mission called Encounter 86, which was held at Bewdley, near Kidderminster. I was asked both to speak at a women's meeting and to give my testimony of healing from cancer at one of the evening meetings.

During that week, Ron was giving a meeting in a pub, and many people were saved and baptised in the Holy Spirit. After the meeting, Ron was approached by a young woman who said she had never seen anything like this in a pub before, and would Ron and I be willing to appear on a Central Television programme called 'Contact'. We agreed to pray about it and we gave the matter much thought. We realised that many people might watch a television programme although they might never go out to a meeting, so this would be an opportunity to take the gospel to those who might otherwise not hear it. It became clear to us that we should accept, for we had both told the Lord that we were willing to do anything and go anywhere for him. So we went to the Central studios and appeared live on 'Contact'. It was a very exciting experience for us, though I did not really feel at home in such glamorous surroundings. Later, another television company made a video of Ron's life story, and I appeared in this briefly. Some of the scenes in this video had to be shot in a prison, and we returned to Rochester in order to make them.

Although my work with Ron and my own ministry was taking me all over the country, and to places I had never imagined I would enter, I was anxious not to neglect my relationships with ordinary local women who I might be able to help. When Ron was away at a conference, I took the opportunity to invite some of the sisters from the church round, asking them to bring unsaved friends. One woman started to ask me about myself and I told her something about my past and how I had met the Lord. She said that she was not a Christian but she could see that we had something that she didn't have. She was a lonely woman, parted from her husband. I talked to her, telling her what Jesus had done for me and could do for her, and she suddenly said, 'I would like to give my heart to the Lord'. We prayed a prayer of repentance and acceptance with her and praised God for her salvation. I rejoice just as much when God uses me to bring one lost sheep to Jesus as when crowds are saved in huge meetings.

The next change that God was to bring about in my life may seem a small thing to some, but to me it was a real miracle. I had never even considered learning to drive. I knew that it was the sort of thing that I would never be able to do; I didn't have the temperament for it. Just to think about it made me feel nervous! But God said to me one day, 'I want you to drive. Get yourself a provisional licence.'

'Who, me?' I said, 'You know I'd never be able to drive, Lord. I'd never have the confidence. I'm too nervous.'

'Put your faith and trust in me,' said the Lord, 'and I can work miracles through you.'

I thought about it. Yes, I believed that God could work miracles through me. Hadn't he healed me from cancer? Hadn't he used me to bring lost souls to himself? But those things seemed easy in comparison with driving! That skill that so many just take for granted seemed an impossibility for me. It would certainly require a miracle.

'All right, Lord,' I said at last, 'if you want me to learn to drive then let a sister come to me with the money for a provisional licence.'

Two weeks later a sister approached me at church. 'Maureen, I felt that the Lord wanted me to give you this,' and she proffered a ten pound note. 'I believe that you should learn to drive and that the Lord wants you to use this for a provisional licence.'

I couldn't reject an answer as dramatic as that, and I sent off for the licence the next day. But the next problem was how I was to afford driving lessons. A brother from the church took me out a couple of times, but didn't really have the confidence to take me on the roads, and we couldn't afford the steep cost of a professional driving instructor. Despite the fact that I was still very nervous about getting behind a wheel, I felt wholly committed to learning to drive now that the Lord had shown me so unmistakably that this was his will for me. I wasn't going to use lack of money as an excuse to give up on the whole idea. I believe that once he saw me stepping out in boldness, God took care of the situation. He saw that I was willing to act, that I was prepared to learn, and he did the rest. A friend approached me and said that he was training to become a driving instructor. He had a dual control car and he would be happy to give me lessons as it would be good practice for him. I would only need to give him a couple of pounds to cover the petrol.

My friend passed his instructor's exam while he was teaching me, but he insisted on taking me through to the test. I began to gain confidence and, as I often told friends, I sometimes felt as though it wasn't me driving at all, but it was the Lord who was in control of the car, as he was in control of this whole situation. This did not prevent me from suffering driving test nerves though, and I failed the first time. The second time, I was still nervous and made a couple of small mistakes, but I felt I had done better. At the end, the examiner turned to me and said, 'Mrs Sims, you did make some mistakes, but I put that down to nerves. I'm going to pass you.'

'Praise the Lord!' I shouted.

'Er, yes,' said the startled examiner, 'I'll give you your pass certificate.'

I sat in the car with my friend and we thanked God for his love and guidance through this period. I am so blessed by the independence and mobility I have gained, and I now actually have my own car. If I needed yet another proof of God's power and goodness, then this was it. If we put our lives in his hands, he can do anything for us, even the impossible.

11: A woman of faith

Ron's ministry grew to such an extent that he began to have difficulties in handling the volume of correspondence and administrative work that arose from it. We were so grateful to God when the leaders of the King's Centre gave Ron a fully equipped office of his own and a secretary to help him deal with the work. Eventually, he formed Ron Sims Ministries, which is an associate organisation of the King's Centre ministries.

Ron and I were both longing for the day when I could give up my job, and devote all my time to working for the Lord, I was already a part of Ron Sims Ministries, but my work was necessarily restricted because of my part-time job and because I still felt that as long as I had a child at school I should be at home for him as much as possible. But as the time for David to leave school approached, I knew that the Lord was telling me to give up my job. This was what I had longed for, but I found that one thing was causing me to hesitate in taking this step. I had been working at the antique shop for twelve years, and it was not going to be easy to tell Mr Lazarus that I was leaving. He had been so good to me, throughout the bad times as well as the good, and we had become friends.

I asked the Lord for guidance and he reassured me that I was doing the right thing. He has all our lives in his hands, and a work for us all to do. Our part is just to love, trust, and obey him. When I told Mr Lazarus that I would be leaving in a month, there were tears in his eyes, and in mine too. I could not help being sad at the thought of leaving this kind man, who had been part of my life for so many years, but I was joyful to know that soon I would be completely free to devote myself to the Lord's work. And with God's perfect timing, I finished work just three days before David's last day at school.

The day I left work, I said to the Lord, 'I am entirely available and I am in your hands for you to lead me wherever you want me to go.' He has certainly kept me busy since then. I almost always accompany Ron wherever he is preaching and he always invites me to minister with him at the end of the meeting, to counsel and pray with those who are in need of help and prayer. I have also been all over the country to lead meetings myself, and I praise God that he has made me a vessel to reach his people. I have seen so many people who are hurting inside, very often because of broken relationships, and it has been wonderful when I have been able to minister the Lord's comfort and healing and have seen lives changed.

Usually I minister only to women, but recently the Lord has shown me that he is able to use me to share his message of salvation and hope to men also. The breakthrough came when I had an invitation to be the guest speaker at the Alton chapter of the Full Gospel Business Men's Fellowship International. Ron had often spoken at FGBMFI meetings, but I never dreamed of being asked, for it was most unusual for them to have a woman speaker. I was very nervous beforehand, saying to the Lord, 'Why ever are you sending me here? How can I speak to all these businessmen? How are they going to respond to me?' The Lord told me: 'I speak through you, so it is the Holy Spirit, not you, that they will be responding to; just go forward in my power.'

Ron accompanied me to the meeting, which started with a meal. I knew that God was with me because, although there were about 100 people present, I felt at ease and not at all nervous. After the meal we sang a few choruses and then I was introduced. As I gave my testimony I felt the Holy Spirit flowing through me, and I was emboldened to make an appeal at the end. I told them how Jesus had suffered agony on the cross and had died so that we might be saved from our sins and healed from our sicknesses. At last I said, 'If there is anyone here who doesn't know the Lord Jesus, I beg you to accept him tonight. This might be your last chance to bring peace and love into your life on earth, and to gain eternal life in heaven. I'd like you all to close your eyes and bow your heads, and if anyone wants to respond to Jesus, will you please put your hand up.'

I looked around and saw that a man right at the back had his hand up. I asked him to come forward so that I could pray for him. When he stood up, I was quite taken aback, for he was enormous – a giant of a man. We prayed the prayer of repentance and Kelvin accepted Jesus into his heart and life. Then we prayed for his baptism in the Holy Spirit and saw Kelvin overcome by the Spirit's power.

Kelvin became a good friend of ours. Although his appearance is so formidable, as soon as he speaks he reveals himself as a very soft and gentle man. He says that he thanks God for my boldness that night, for it has changed his life. When Kelvin came to the Lord he was a very lonely and unhappy man as his marriage had broken down. He had parted from his wife and son and was living in digs. Whenever he came round to us we would pray for reconciliation in his marriage and we praise God that he is now back with his wife and they have recently had a little girl. Kelvin is such a lovely Christian, always enthusing about Jesus and what he has done for him. I count it a privilege to have been used as God's instrument in the life of such a man.

Because of our broken first marriages, and the mess we had made of our own marriage in our old life, Ron and I have a particular concern for marriage and families.

We are always so happy when we can be used in Jesus' work of reconciliation in family relationships. Kelvin's was just one of several cases where I was used in this way. At a women's meeting that I had addressed, one of the women who had given their lives to Jesus that day spoke to me afterwards. She told me that she had two children and her husband had left her six months before. She had no idea where he was now and no one to turn to.

'I still love him very much,' she said. 'I get so depressed sometimes. In fact only yesterday I was thinking about ending it all.'

'But you have accepted Jesus now,' I said. 'He is going to help you in every situation. We're going to pray now that you will find your husband and that your family will be reunited. Once we've prayed then all you have to do is to have faith that Jesus will deal with the situation. You can just let go and leave it all to him.'

As we prayed, she wept. And afterwards she said that she had felt all the stress and strain of the last few months leaving her. I could see for myself that this was true, for she immediately looked better. She had been pale and drawn, and now looked healthy and relaxed. Some months later I met the same woman at another meeting. She approached me eagerly, all smiles.

'Maureen, I'm so glad to see you. When I left you that day I went home feeling I was on cloud nine. I started reading my Bible straight away. I was sure Jesus would help me, like you said, and sure enough I heard from a friend who knew where my husband was. He's in Winchester serving a sentence for robbery. But I've been to see him there and we've agreed that as soon as he comes out he's coming home and we're going to try to make a go of our marriage.'

I was so happy for her, though I was not surprised, for I have seen so many prayers answered, so many needs met, once people are prepared to hand over their problems to the Lord.

I had wonderful experience of God's work of re-conciliation in my own life. One Sunday evening I was sitting in the King's Centre when a sister came up to me and said, 'Maureen, there's a woman sitting at the back who wants to see you. She says she knew you and Ron before you were Christians.'

'What's her name?' I asked, full of curiosity.

'Karen,' my friend said, and my heart sank. This was the wife of the couple with whom we had been involved in wife-swapping all those years ago. Though both her husband and I had been reluctant to participate in the arrangement, Karen and Ron had been very enthusiastic and I knew she had wanted Ron to go away with her. Did I really want to face this woman again? Then I thought about how it would be for her, having to face me. Surely she would be feeling guilty and uncomfort-able. I followed my friend to the back of the church.

I went straight up to Karen and hugged her, for I wanted her to know that I had forgiven her. As soon as I saw her I had realised that I would have no prob-lems about forgiveness. Jesus had taken away all the old jealousy and hatred, and I had nothing but love for Karen in my heart now. I invited her over for tea with her two children, and found that we were able to get on well together. We were even able to talk over the past without my experiencing any hurt, or any recurrence of hostile feelings towards her. I saw Karen a few times after that, and we parted as friends. Jesus tells us, in Matthew chapter 5, verse 44, to 'love your enemies and pray for those who persecute you'. This is a very hard commandment for mere human nature to obey, but if we let Jesus take control he will deal with all our hatred and resentments and it becomes easy to love and forgive those who have harmed us.

I have never been afraid to talk freely about my past. When I give my testimony, women often say to me afterwards, 'Maureen, how can you talk about those things? How can you be so open? Doesn't it hurt you?'

I tell them that my past life is no longer any part of the new creation that is Maureen Sims today. My past sins are forgiven but they should not be forgotten, because talking about them might be able to bring release and new life to others.

Over the years, and especially after Ron's book *Flying Free* was published, many people have been put in touch with us in the hope that we could help them. We have had people coming to our house for counselling who have been involved in the same sordid life that we once knew: crime, drugs, drink, prostitution, pornography. If we were not perfectly honest about our own past involvement these people would not be able to identify with us, and we would not be able to help them. And, whenever I speak in public, I am aware that somewhere among the listeners there might be a woman who is suffering the sort of miseries and living the sort of life that was once mine. In obedience to Jesus, I feel I must be open about my past so that any woman in such a situation might realise that if God could bring release and forgiveness to a sinner like me, then he can do it for her too, if she is willing to accept Jesus as her Lord and Saviour.

One of my greatest desires, and one that I am optimistic will soon be realised, is to be allowed to minister in a woman's prison. My heart reaches out to the women there, for I could so easily have been in their place, but for God's grace. I want to show them that God lifted me up from sin and degradation, and gave me new life and hope, and he can do the same for 'the vilest offender who truly believes'.

One of the ways in which the Lord has used Ron and myself over the years is as a channel of his healing powers. We have seen many wonderful instances of healing, and yet we have a health problem ourselves, for Ron still suffers from angina and other difficulties with his heart.

His strength and stamina has grown, and his schedule of work and travelling would be daunting to many healthy men, but nevertheless the problem remains.

Ron has been prayed for and at one time we did believe that he had been completely healed and that the Lord had given him a new heart. But at the end of 1986 he had a very bad relapse. We think it is no coincidence that this happened at a time when Ron was at a spiritual low. He had been listening to others instead of to Jesus, and had become dispirited because of negative criticism from other Christians. He had let bitterness creep into his heart, and just after Christmas he was taken into hospital with a massive heart attack. Once more his life was in the gravest danger, but we praise God, for he spared it yet again. Ron was able to return to his ministry having learned the valuable lesson that we must keep our eyes fixed firmly on Jesus, who will never let us down, and not become dependent on the praise and approval of others.

Since that, Ron and I have often tried to understand the strange situation whereby Jesus could use Ron to touch others with his healing, but despite many prayers he seemed to be unwilling to heal Ron's own illness. Then while praying together we received a Scripture from the Lord in answer. It was 2 Corinthians, chapter 12, verses 7 to 10, where the apostle Paul says:

And to keep me from being too elated by the abundance of revelations, a thorn was given me in the flesh, a messenger of Satan, to harass me, to keep me from being too elated. Three times I besought the Lord about this, that it should leave me, but he said to me, 'My grace is sufficient for you, for my power is made perfect in weakness.' I will all the more gladly boast of my weaknesses, that the power of Christ may rest upon me. For the sake of Christ, then, I am content with weaknesses, hardships, persecutions, and calamities; for when I am weak, then I am strong.

We understood from this Scripture that, just as the Lord had called Paul to a special ministry, he had called Ron, and this thorn in Ron's flesh was God's way of keeping him humble and reliant on the Lord. But we believe that by his grace, God can keep Ron in health to do his work for many years to come.

One of the loveliest ways in which God has blessed us in recent years is through reuniting us with our families. One night in the spring of 1987, when Ron was preaching in Wales, he was approached by a young woman after the service. 'Hello Dad,' she said, and Ron realised that it was his daughter Tina, with whom we had lost touch.

'Tina!' he cried, hugging her. 'How did you know I was going to be here tonight?'

'There was a bit about the meeting in the local paper,' she told him, 'and I didn't want to miss seeing my dad preaching.'

We went back to Tina's house and met her family. She had three children now, and Ron was delighted to see these grandchildren he had not known existed. It turned out, in fact, that Ron was actually the grandfather of eleven children, for his sons had married and had families. But we were sad to learn that Tina's brothers had all been in various kinds of trouble, and that John and Mike were both in prison on remand, awaiting trial for robberies. The next day we were able to visit John in Cardiff Prison, and we told him about the love and salvation of Jesus. Ron was very moved to see his son, for he reminded him so much of his old self.

We have kept in touch with Ron's first family since then, exchanging letters with John and Mike, and having his oldest son Steven to stay with us. Steven says that he is sick of his old life and he has made a commitment to Jesus. He is finding it hard to readjust and shake off old habits, but we trust that God will bring him through. Both the younger boys are looking for the truth, and Mike in particular shows signs of accepting Jesus as his Saviour. We believe that God is working in the hearts of all four of them and they will be reunited, not just to their earthly father, but to their heavenly father.

I, too, have known the joy of a family reunion. Recently my first son, Garry, has been in contact with my mother, and she has brought us together. He came over to stay for a weekend with my mum, and met all my family. It was wonderful to see how well he got on with his brother Graham, who he had not seen for so many years. His half-brothers Michael and David were complete strangers to him of course, but in no time they became the best of friends. As to his relationship with Ron, Garry bears no grudges, and thinks the world of his stepfather now. I feel he is a son to be proud of, for he has grown into a lovely man, caring and sensitive, though he takes after me in being very quiet. We pray that he, too, will come to know and accept the Lord Jesus, and of course we continue to pray the same for my dear mother, who has stood by me so loyally throughout the years.

God says in his word, 'I will restore to you the years that the locusts have eaten' (Joel 2:25). Ron and I believe that God has honoured our trust and obedience by restoring to us the families that we lost in those dark years that are now behind us.

I have so much to thank Jesus for that I don't know where to start in praising him for his goodness to me. Even in my old life I can see his loving hand upon me, and since I have known him as my Lord he has guided me every step of the way. I praise him for my good health, my loving husband, my wonderful sons, and the wealth of brothers and sisters in the Lord who give me so much love and support. For so many years I longed for love and looked for it in vain. Now I am blessed with a superabundance of loving relationships: with Ron, with family and friends, and with my Lord who loves me as no one else can.

I praise Jesus too for the strength he has given me, the power to step forward in boldness to do his will and his work. I know that no one is too weak or too insignificant to have a job to do for the Lord. No one could have been weaker than I was, a mere zombie with no mind of my own, too shy and stupid to talk to anyone. But God has created a strong new Maureen Sims who is a woman of faith and boldness, a woman who is not afraid to stand in front of hundreds of people to testify to God's goodness and greatness.

It has been such a privilege to be used by God as a channel of his love, salvation and healing. It has been wonderful to travel the country with Ron, either supporting him in his ministry, or receiving his loving support when I am speaking. We have witnessed many signs and wonders over the years. But of all the miracles that I have witnessed, I still feel that the greatest miracle is to see lives changed, to see men, women, and young people being born anew to fulness of life in Jesus Christ.

I still cannot see Ron preaching without feeling a thrill of pride that God should use my husband to minister his gospel so powerfully. And sometimes I look at Ron, and see him look at me with such love and tenderness, and I can hardly believe that this is the same man I married. I just break down in tears of happiness and thankfulness for the life that we have together now.

Just as people are sometimes surprised by my openness about my past, they are often shocked by the frankness with which I describe the old Ron. 'How can you talk about your husband like that?' I have sometimes been asked. But I persist in being honest, for Ron and I want people to realise the full extent of the miracle that Jesus has brought about in our lives. Ron was an evil man, a hard and bitter man. Prison couldn't break him, near-fatal illness couldn't break him, but Jesus Christ reached out to him with forgiveness and salvation and brought him to his knees. Jesus died for sinners, and there is nobody who is beyond the reach of his love and redemption.

Like Ron, I have been forgiven much. It may seem as though I was only a victim, the unwilling partner in our shameful life together. But I cannot protest total innocence. Yes, I was weak, I was stupid, I was led astray. But I, too, was a lost sinner, a prisoner of Satan, bound in his chains. Satan seeks to imprison us all, to rob and destroy us, and the only hope we have is in Jesus. Only Jesus can save us from Satan. Only Jesus can break the chains that bind us and set us free, as he set Ron and me free.

My dearest wish is that this book will reach people and give them hope. It has not been easy to tell my story, but it will have been worth it if it brings encouragement and hope in Jesus to anyone's life. I want everyone to know that we must never give up hope in salvation. Whatever your past you can be forgiven and given new life. Don't give up hope about your unsaved wife, husband, or parents; don't feel that your rebellious son or daughter is beyond help. Ron and I have proved so often in our lives that 'nothing is impossible in God through Christ Jesus'.

Ron and I glory in the knowledge that the old life is behind us and we are living as new creations. I am not Maureen Sims the ex-prostitute; he is not Ron Sims the ex-convict, the ex-porn king. Whatever we may have been in the past, we are now a prince and a princess. For we are the son and daughter of the King of kings and Lord of lords. All glory to his precious name!